Infant/Toddler Caregiving

A Guide to

Setting Up

Environments

Second Edition

J. Ronald Lally, Jay Stewart,
and Deborah Greenwald

Developed collaboratively by the
California Department of Education
and WestEd

  WestEd

Publishing Information

Infant/Toddler Caregiving: A Guide to Setting Up Environments
(Second Edition) was developed by the WestEd Center for Child and
Family Studies, Sausalito. It was edited by Faye Ong, working in
cooperation with Tom Cole, Consultant, Quality Improvement Office.
It was prepared for printing by the staff of CDE Press; the cover and
interior design were created and prepared by Cheryl McDonald; type-
setting was done by Jeannette Reyes. It was published by the Department,
1430 N Street, Sacramento, CA 95814-5901. It was distributed under the
provisions of the Library Distribution Act and *Government Code* Section
11096.

ISBN 978-8011-1701-5

Ordering Information

Copies of this publication are available for sale from the California
Department of Education (CDE). For prices and ordering information on
products from the Program for Infant/Toddler Care, please go http://www.
wested.org. The *Educational Resource Catalog* is at http://www.cde.
ca.gov/re/pn/rc or call the CDE Press Sales Office at 1-800-995-4099.
The catalog describes publications, videos, and other instructional media
available from the CDE.

Notice

The guidance in *Infant/Toddler Caregiving: A Guide to Setting Up
Environments* (Second Edition) is not binding on local educational
agencies or other entities. Except for the statutes, regulations, and court
decisions that are referenced herein, the documents is exemplary, and
compliance with it is not mandatory. (See *Education Code* Section
33308.5.)

Contents

Message from the State Superintendent of Public Instruction   v
About the Authors   vii
Acknowledgments   ix
Introduction   1

Section One
Creating Environments for Infants and Toddlers—Key Concepts   6

    Safety   6
    Health   8
    Comfort   10
    Convenience   11
    Child Size   13
    Flexibility   14
    Movement   14
    Choice   15

Section Two
Planning Your Infant/Toddler Care Setting   17

    Environments and Different Age Groups   18
    Relationship-based Care   21
    Family Child Care and Center Care   26
    Division and Definition of Space   28

Section Three
Setting Up Specific Areas   36

    Entrance and Family Communication Area   36
    Learning and Development Centers   37
    Peer Play Areas   43
    Multilevel Areas   45
    Rest and Sleeping Areas   47
    Toileting, Washing Up, Mealtime, and Food Preparation Areas   49
    Storage and Shelves   52
    Outdoor Space   55

Section Four

Accommodations for Children with Disabilities or Other Special Needs 61

Physical Disabilities (Orthopedic Impairments)   61
Visual Impairments   62
Hearing Impairments   63
Emotional or Behavioral Challenges   63
Developmental Disabilities   64
Create Multisensory Experiences   64
Capitalize on Strengths   64
Allow for Extra Time and Repeated Practice   65

Section Five

Practical Tips   66

Air, Light, and Heating   66
Boxes and Barrels   66
Carpets   67
Ceilings   67
Changeable Environment   67
Cleanliness   68
Cushions   68
Floor Surfaces   68
Custodial Support   68
Light and Texture Variations   68
Limited Space   69
Overstimulation   69
Home Away from Home   69

Suggested Resources   70
Glossary   76

A Message from the State Superintendent of Public Instruction

At a time when over half the mothers in this country are gainfully employed, most of them full time, more young children require care outside the home than ever before. Although an increasing number of child care services have struggled to keep pace with the rapidly increasing demand, appropriate care for young children remains difficult for families to find. Training is crucial to increase the number of quality child care programs. The Child Development Division of the California Department of Education has an innovative and comprehensive approach to training infant care teachers and program leaders called the Program for Infant/Toddler Care (PITC). The PITC has gained national and international acclaim since its inception in 1986 and offers a comprehensive training system consisting of a series of training DVDs, a series of infant care teacher guides, and trainer's manuals. All DVDs have Spanish editions, and all trainer's manuals are also available in Spanish.

The purpose of the infant care teacher guides is to offer information based on current theory, research, and practice to teachers in both centers and family child care homes. Each guide addresses an area of infant development and care, covering major issues of concern and related practical considerations, including the care of infants and toddlers with disabilities or other special needs. The guides provide extensive and in-depth coverage of a topic and are intended to be used with the DVDs, which illustrate key concepts and caregiving techniques for a specific area of care.

Like the other guides in the PITC series, this one is rich in practical guidelines and suggestions. The ideas presented in this document are intended to help infant care teachers set up environments that promote young children's health, safety, and comfort; meet their developmental needs and interests; and provide a comfortable and convenient place for the teacher to work.

This second edition offers expanded information on how environments support the high-quality, relationship-based care espoused by the PITC. A well-designed infant/toddler care environment plays an essential role in facilitating the intimate relationship between an infant care teacher and an infant or toddler. The second edition gives special attention to the PITC policy of continuity of care. This relationship-based policy aims to keep children and teachers together in care for three years. Examples are provided of programs designed to support and protect continuity of care and close relationships between teachers and children and between children. The emphasis on relationships includes sensitivity to differences.

This edition has information on how to recognize and respond to cultural differences and family preferences in the context of the environment. Additional information is provided on the care of infants and toddlers with disabilities or other special needs in inclusive settings. This edition features strategies for arranging and adapting the environment. Newer terms replace older ones, for example, *infant care teacher* in place of *caregiver* and *program leader* in place of *administrator, director,* and *family child care operator.* New terminology is defined in the Glossary.

JACK O'CONNELL
State Superintendent of Public Instruction

About the Authors

J Ronald Lally, Ph.D., is the co-director of the Center for Child and Family Studies at WestEd, an educational research, development, and service organization in Sausalito. He received his doctorate in educational psychology from the University of Florida in 1968, and a postdoctoral certificate in infant testing from the Child Development Research Centre in London in the same year. For many years, he was a professor at Syracuse University and chair of its Department of Child and Family Studies. He has been involved in developing programs and policies for young children and their families since 1966.

For the past 20 years, he has directed the work of the Program for Infant/Toddler Care, a collaboration between the California Department of Education and WestEd. The DVD and print products of the program are the most widely distributed infant/toddler care training materials in the world. Intensive train-the-trainer relationships have also been established with 15 states in addition to California. Most recently, he and his staff have been responsible for the development of infant/toddler and preschool guidelines and standards for the states of California and Ohio, and he has advised government agencies on infant/toddler issues.

Dr. Lally has been active in the development and operation of Early Head Start. He served on the Health and Human Services Advisory Committee on Services for Families with Infants and Toddlers that developed Early Head Start. He is on the National Advisory Committees of the Ounce of Prevention Fund, the Nova/Southeastern University Family Center, the Hilton Early Head Start Special Quest, and Stop Crime: Invest In Kids. He is on the board of directors and one of the founders of Zero to Three, National Center for Infants, Toddlers, and Families.

Jay Stewart is an editor and freelance writer. Much of her work has been in the fields of psychology and education. She has collaborated on books dealing with a variety of subjects, including cancer prevention and the needs of children with disabilities.

Deborah Greenwald directed the development of the California Department of Education's *Infant/Toddler Learning and Development Program Guidelines* (2006) as well as the *Infant/Toddler Learning and Development Program Guidelines: The Workbook* (2009). Ms. Greenwald is a faculty member of the Program for Infant/Toddler Care Institutes. Prior to working at WestEd, she spent 15 years in infant/toddler group care. She also taught parent/infant guidance classes and was an infant/toddler trainer in a resource and referral agency.

Ms. Greenwald received a B.A. in child development from Humboldt State University and an M.A. in human development from Pacific Oaks College. She also holds a certificate from the American Montessori Society and is an associate of Resources for Infant Educarers.

Acknowledgments

The first edition of this publication was developed by the WestEd Center for Child and Family Studies, under the direction of J. Ronald Lally. The developers are indebted to Joan Bergstrom, Jerry Fergusen, Jim Greenman, Anita Olds, Janet Poole, Craig Ramey, Mary Smithberger, Louis Torelli, and Yolanda Torres for their participation in intensive content interviews, which greatly contributed to the content of that document. Special thanks go to Louis Torelli, who was responsible for the selection and design of the illustrations, and to Peter Mangione and Sheila Signer, who played a major role in the writing of that edition.

A special note of gratitude goes to the members of the California and national review panels for work on the first edition. The California panel members were Dorlene Clayton, Dee Cuney, Ronda Garcia, Jacquelyne Jackson, Lee McKay, Janet Nielsen, Pearlene Reese, Maria Ruiz, June Sale, Patty Siegel, and Lenore Thompson. The national panel members were T. Berry Brazelton, Laura Dittman, Richard Fiene, Magda Gerber, Asa Hilliard, Alice Honig, Jeree Pawl, Sally Provence, Eleanor Szanton, Bernice Weissbourd, and Donna Wittmer.

Deborah Greenwald revised the guide and developed the second edition under the direction of J. Ronald Lally and Peter L. Mangione, co-directors of the Center for Child and Family Studies, WestEd, which developed of the Program for Infant/Toddler Care, in collaboration with the California Department of Education, Child Development Division. Special thanks are due to contributing writers and advisers for this project: Debbie Bergstrom, Linda Brault, Judy Calder, Caren Calhoun, Mary Jane Chainski, Joe Lang, Cheryl Oku, Sheila Signer, Louis Torelli, and Mary Smithberger and the Child Development Division, California Department of Education, for their review and recommendations on content. Sylvia Stein Wright provided editorial assistance.

Sara Webb Schmitz provided example 1, and Apurva Dave provided example 2 on page 1.

The following programs deserve appreciation for allowing photographs of their sites to be taken for the second edition of this publication:

ASI Early Childhood Education Center, San Francisco State University,
   San Francisco
Associated Students' Children's Center, California State University, Sacramento
BlueSkies for Children, Oakland
Chabot College Children's Center

Child Development Center, Merced College, Merced
Eben-Ezer Family Child Care, San Francisco
Educare, Omaha, Nebraska
Fifth Avenue Early Head Start, San Rafael
King Family Child Care
Marin Head Start, Hamilton
Marin Head Start, Meadowpark
Marin Head Start, Fifth Avenue
Presidio Child Development Center, San Francisco
South of Market Child Care, Inc., San Francisco
UCLA Megan E. Daly Infant Development Program

Introduction

When you walk into a quiet hospital room, you start whispering. But when you enter a crowded gymnasium to watch a basketball game, you have to yell at the person next to you to make room for you to sit. Your personality has not changed, but the environment has. How you feel, what you do, and how you respond all depend on where you are:

- In some settings, you feel relaxed, comfortable, and free to open up and be yourself.
- In other places, you feel formal, stiff, and slightly on guard.

The environments in which people live and work convey messages about what is okay and what is not, what is expected or allowed, and what is encouraged. Indeed, whether the people who create environments are aware of it or not, every environment conveys messages. For instance, if you enter a room that has furnishings, music, and scents similar to your childhood home, you would probably feel comfortable. Conversely, if everything in a room is unusual to you, from the furnishings to the language(s) spoken, you would probably feel discomfort.

Surroundings such as those in examples 1 and 2 have an effect on adults. For babies who cannot crawl or walk and are captive in the environments, the effect may be even more powerful. Young infants cannot move to another room or rearrange the setting. They are forced to see, touch, smell, feel, and hear whatever is around them at the moment or "tune out" the environment.

Infants and toddlers learn about and experience life through sensory and motor explorations. They touch, taste, smell, observe, and move the world about them to make sense out of it. Children from birth to three years of age live directly through their senses. Adults, for example, have an image of how a chair should look and

1

2

1

compare new chairs with that image while infants form an image from their first contact with a chair. Therefore the environment in which infants are placed has a tremendous impact. What they see, hear, taste, and touch create strong impressions. The type and number of people around infants influence how the children feel about relationships.

Relationships, above all, characterize an infant/toddler care setting. Even as environments for infants and toddlers are described, every aspect of the environment is part of the critical support system that helps infant care teachers develop close, caring relationships with small groups of infants and toddlers in their care. A cozy chair big enough for an infant care teacher and one or two children to snuggle and read, a small table where a teacher and small group of toddlers can eat together, even a tire swing that a few children can use at once—all suggest and support a sense of togetherness for the infants, toddlers, family members, and teachers who use the environment. A well-designed environment sets the tone for intimacy.

A child care environment is not neutral. It is one of the child's most valuable teachers. The space a child inhabits and moves in minute by minute and day after day introduces the child to the colors, shapes, smells, and sounds of the world. It also introduces him to the places where people feel welcome, meet, rest, and eat. When these experiences are familiar ones, similar to the child's home, the environment can help an infant feel safe and connected to the place. Yet those who create child care settings, often unknowingly, develop environments that are familiar to them and based on their own cultural practices rather than the practices of the children and families they serve. When the child care environment is dramatically different from the home, the child

may have to struggle to adapt. Therefore it is important for infant care teachers and program leaders to consciously consider the cultural context of their environments and the cultural messages their program sends. Program staff members and family members can work collaboratively to create familiar settings and experiences for the children. Connecting the look and feel of the child care environment to experiences that children have at home should be a high priority.

Infants and toddlers grow and learn by interacting with their environment, including people, and watching what happens. As they explore, infants discover the effects of certain actions:

- A fall on the linoleum floor—a hard surface
- Crawling on a rug—a soft surface
- Touching a ball—movement
- Pushing a big rock—no movement
- Pushing a toddler—being pushed back

Understanding and growth follow those discoveries; for example, pillows are soft and fun to fall on, but a fall on the hard floor hurts.

Infants and toddlers build concepts based on their sensory and motor explorations. For example, they learn the difference between wet and dry, soft and hard, rough and smooth, cold and hot, movable and stationary. Even when a child has a disability or other special needs, he or she builds concepts through sensory and motor experiences in the environment. You may need to support the child to explore the environment. For example, a child with limited use of his hands may need more assistance in reaching for items to explore. This is just one example. Examples of different ways to adapt the environment and support a child with special needs will be provided throughout this guide. Always check with family members and specialists involved with the child for appropriate ideas.

The floors, ceiling, lighting, walls, and furniture all contribute to the infants' and toddlers' education about the world. By making choices and interacting freely with their surroundings, infants and toddlers can follow their interests and try out their developing abilities. For instance, when a young infant has a safe space on a firm, padded floor to kick her legs, roll from side to side, and grasp at objects, she is able to follow her own impulses to move, learn from her experiences, and adapt her movements to become more coordinated over time. Today the young toddler can take more steps; next the toddler can go from the couch to the chair. The child is not only mastering a new skill, but also learning more about who he or she is and what he or she can do.

The environment also affects you, the infant care teacher. A totally child-centered environment should not be your goal. An excellent setting for infant/toddler care accommodates the needs of the teachers as well as those of the infants and toddlers. However, the following problems may result from an environment that is not carefully set up:

- If the environment makes you anxious about the children's safety, you cannot relax and play with the children.
- If the room arrangement does not allow you to find things easily, you get frustrated and waste precious time.
- If you do not have a place to relax away from the children for a few moments, you may experience burnout.
- If the environment is not set up conveniently for daily routines, you may feel fatigue and frustration.
- If adults in the environment have no place to sit or no support for getting up from the floor, family members may not feel welcome, and teachers may be at risk for injuries.

You need a place that is comfortable for you and that supports your work. The caregiving environment must meet your needs *and* the children's, so both you and the children can relax and enjoy one another. In an interview in *Beginnings* (1984), Jim Greenman, an infant environment expert, stated: "Infant and toddler rooms should spark the response: *What a neat place to be a little kid! What a neat place to be WITH a little kid!*"

Making an infant care environment a "neat place to be" takes planning. The setting should engage the infants' large and small muscles, captivate their senses, and activate their curiosity. Infants need to be cared for in places that are safe *and* interesting. The environment should also make the young child feel secure and free from danger. This publication will help you promote those environmental characteristics. Each section looks at environments from a

3

different point of view and provides suggestions from that perspective.

Section One identifies and describes eight key concepts that need to be considered in the design of a child care environment. The concepts allow you to look at the same piece of equipment or room arrangement plan from eight different viewpoints to make sure that the infants' best interests are considered. In addition to defining each concept, the section suggests practical steps to improve certain features of the environment. Taken together, the eight concepts will help you focus on the entire environment and its overall impact on both adults and children alike. (The DVD *Space to Grow: Creating a Child Care Environment for Infants and Toddlers* [2004], has useful ideas.)

Section Two considers those aspects of the environment that make each setting unique and suggests how to work with that uniqueness in environmental planning. In this section, you can look at the environment through the lens of the six PITC essential policies for relationship-based care. The section provides a framework for looking at your own particular environment. Characteristics of the program that clarify the purpose, constraints, possibilities, and potential impact of an environment on infants, toddlers, and teachers are discussed. Some characteristics are more obvious than others. For example, the age of the children in the program will make a difference. A related issue is the composition of the group by age—that is, whether children are grouped together with others close in age, separate from other age groups, or mixed with children of various ages. Another obvious factor is whether the program is a family child care home or an infant/toddler center.

Among the more subtle elements of a setting is the location of pathways for movement. The potential location of open space in the environment and access to outdoor areas are additional considerations. Another consideration is how the environment influences opportunities for intimacy and connections between people. Each setting and program is going to differ. The recommendations are general guidelines; compliance with state and local rules and regulations is important when changes are made to your environment.

This section will help you carry out the planning necessary to make the most of the environment for yourself and for the infants and toddlers in your care. Looking at the environment from different perspectives can help you to see how aspects of environmental design, such as the placement of a sink, can make a big difference to program quality for infants, toddlers, their families, and their infant care teachers.

Section Three explores specific areas of the child care environment. For example, if you want ideas about how to set up the food preparation area, you can skip ahead to that topic in the section. There you will find detailed information on how to set up the area as well as how it relates to the eight key concepts described in Section One. Section Three is rich in illustrations that are reinforced in the text and vice versa. Much of the detail in the third section is devoted to practical concerns—for example, what kinds of materials to use in building a small play structure or in creating a textured pathway.

The strategies in this guide are meant for all infants and toddlers, including those with disabilities or other special needs. Throughout the guide, specific examples and ideas are offered to show how a disability may be accommodated. Section Five provides practical tips specific to children with physical disabilities. However, when you are determining how to

adapt the environment or activity for a child in your program, it is best to work closely with the child's family and any specialists who may be working with the child. Children do not fit into neat categories, and children with disabilities are not defined by their disability. Adaptations, including the use of adaptive materials or equipment, modified interactions and expectations, and planning, will often be most effective. Start with what is best for all children.

The guide closes with practical tips, suggested resources, and a Glossary of environmental terms. Some tips are general, and others are quite specific. Some refer to the entire environment, and others refer to a specific area. The practical tips provide additional detail. The list of suggested resources is provided for readers seeking additional information on environmental topics. Because much of the terminology on the topic of environments is technical, a Glossary is provided. It will help you find a definition of a term quickly. The Glossary also can be used as a learning tool. Extensive definitions explain concepts and ideas with examples. For the reader who wants to become familiar with the terminology related to environments and who wants to pick up some interesting ideas along the way, the Glossary is a good place to start.

Section One:
Creating Environments for Infants and Toddlers—Key Concepts

One of the best ways to make sure that you are meeting the needs of the infants and toddlers you serve is to develop an understanding of the key concepts to be considered in the creation of a caregiving environment. The research for this guide and the corresponding DVD, *Space to Grow* (2004), led to the discovery of numerous important and useful concepts. Of these, eight were selected as key concepts. These eight important environmental qualities sometimes deal with the same piece of equipment or environmental area, but each concept gives a unique perspective for environmental design. Decisions about the environment should be made after you have analyzed the impact of the environment on all eight of the key concepts, not just one or two. In other words, those eight qualities are the building blocks for environmental planning. With each concept, you will also want to ensure access for children and/or adults with disabilities or other special needs. The infant/toddler caregiving environment should:

1. Ensure *safety*
2. Promote *health*
3. Provide *comfort*
4. Be *convenient*
5. Be *child-sized*
6. Maximize *flexibility*
7. Encourage *movement*
8. Allow for *choice*

Safety

In a safe setting, infants and toddlers are free to move and explore. They can make their own choices. You do not worry, police, or referee as much. A safe environment allows you to relax and watch or play with the children. You do not have to say no as often when you are in a safe setting.

Here are some things to do so the children will be safe while they are being active:

- Cover electrical outlets.
- Remove things that break easily.
- Put guards around radiators, hot pipes, and other hot surfaces.
- Use carpet padding under carpets to cushion falls.
- Use low-pile carpets that make clean-up easy and small objects visible.
- Remove trip hazards for adults and children.
- Choose nontoxic materials and furnishings.

- Use Integrated Pest Management techniques to control pests and infestations. (See the Suggested Resources section for more information.)
- Keep rocking chairs and furniture with sharp corners out of frequently used pathways. Make sure that the floor space where young children often walk or crawl is kept clear.
- Install gates in front of stairways.
- Fence the outside play area with gates that children cannot open.
- Use diaper tables with a 3- to 6-inch raised edge to prevent infants from rolling off and falling.
- Place recommended shock-absorbing materials under indoor or outdoor climbing equipment.
- Check to see that all equipment meets consumer standards. Stay informed about product recalls or safety alerts.
- Store all medications in recommended lock boxes to prevent access by children or other unauthorized persons.
- Remove any plants that are poisonous, irritating, or dangerous to touch or fall into.
- Remove choking hazards such as small objects, dropped pieces of food, and loose cords or ropes; modify cords used in opening window shades or curtains to eliminate any choking hazard.
- Maintain unobstructed exits for safe and speedy evacuation in case of an emergency.

Removal of Hazards

Remove appliances with electric cords that can be pulled off surfaces such as a counter, high shelf, or adult-sized table. Remove other hazards, such as chipped paint, loose pieces of tile, unscreened heaters, unstable shelves, broken toys and equipment, buckets or tubs of water, and anything with sharp edges. Remove and store household products, such as cleaners, chemicals, medicines, and cosmetics, in high places and locked cabinets. Be sure that no buckets or containers of water are left where children have access to them without close supervision.

After you remove hazards, you can more confidently let infants explore freely. Setting up a safe environment frees you from worry, so you feel more secure. However, toddlers can often find ways to get to hazardous equipment and materials you may think are safely out of reach. Always be aware of potential hazards that can be reached by an infant developing new skills.

Safety Checks

A great way to see if a room is safe for infants and toddlers is to get down and look around from the child's level. Ask yourself:

- Are there places a small hand or head could get caught?
- Are there stairs or ledges too steep for a safe tumble?
- Do any sharp corners or awkward room arrangements cause problems?

Illustration by Paul Lee

- Do crawling infants and toddlers have safe, clear pathways with no obstacles?
- Do the traffic patterns provide protection for children who are not independently mobile?
- Can infants and toddlers exercise all body parts, roll, crawl, climb, slide, and run and still be safe?
- If you have a child with a disability or other special need, additional checks may be needed. For example, if a child is visually impaired, is furniture in the expected place? If a child uses a therapeutic walker, is the lip between the carpeting and tiled areas smooth and flat?

Health

A healthful setting reduces the chance of contracting or spreading illness and boosts everyone's physical and emotional well-being. Establishing and maintaining a healthful setting should be your goal. Health and safety policies and practices should be clearly defined in written policies, guidelines, and statements that are reviewed periodically and revised as necessary to ensure that they are appropriate for *all* children being served. For example, sanitation procedures may need to be even more stringent when you care for infants and toddlers who are medically fragile. Remember that children cared for in small groups tend to have fewer colds and common illnesses than children in larger groups.

The California Child Care Health Line is a useful resource for any questions you may have about children's health in child care settings (1-800-333-3212). Another option is the National Resource Center for Health and Safety in Child Care and Early Education at the University of Colorado. The center was developed to promote safety in child care settings nationally. By calling a "warmline" (1-800-598-KIDS

[5437]), people can find child care health and safety information. *Caring for Our Children: National Health and Safety Performance Standards Guidelines for Out-of-Home Child Care Programs* (2002) is a helpful publication. The center also developed a Web resource for parents of children who attend child care: Healthy Kids, Healthy Care (http://www.healthykids.us).

Heat, Light, and Ventilation

The first step in creating a healthful environment is to check the heat, lighting, and fresh air supply. Make sure the child care space has enough heat, humidity, light, and ventilation—especially at floor level, where infants and toddlers spend most of their time. Check the lighting carefully. Good lighting affects how people feel and supports health. Everyone needs some exposure to natural light to stay healthy.

Cleanliness

Cleanliness can help prevent sickness and keep it from spreading. The following practices are essential:

- Separate the diapering, food preparation, and feeding areas.
- Ensure that both children's and adults' sinks have hot and cold water in both the changing and feeding areas. Children's sinks should have a mixing valve to regulate the water temperature, which should not exceed 110 degrees Fahrenheit.
- Use easy-to-clean materials when creating the changing and feeding areas.
- Clean the food preparation, feeding, and toileting areas after each use.
- Have a regular schedule for cleaning and sanitizing walls, floors, rugs, bedding, and all toys and equipment. Check for broken toys, equipment, and other hazardous conditions while you clean.

- Set up a regular maintenance schedule for cleaning the furnace and for replacing filters to keep the air fresh.
- Install a humidifier if the air is too dry.
- Check the labels on all pillows, toys, carpets, and mattresses at the time of purchase to make sure they are made from hypoallergenic materials.
- Place washable covers on all pillows and cushions.

Furnishings and Materials

Consider health issues whenever you choose furnishings, equipment, or materials. Ask yourself:

- Can these pillows and mattresses be protected with waterproof covers?
- Can pillow covers be removed easily and washed?

- Is this couch easy to clean?
- Can these mats be fitted with washable covers?
- Is this rug made of material that promotes health? Is it washable, nonslip, and hypoallergenic?
- Is a hand-washing sink readily available for children and teachers to wash their hands regularly?
- Are any bare light bulbs visible that could cause eyestrain, especially for infants who often gaze upwards?
- Would the use of a dishwasher, washing machine, and dryer be efficient?
- Are cleaning products labeled and stored in their original containers and used safely?
- Are art materials nontoxic?
- If children or adults have special health care needs, are the materials certified for use without risk of health hazards by anyone, including children?

Overstimulation

Overstimulation can be a health hazard and is often overlooked. Are the walls, floors, and furniture in a color soothing to the eye and not distracting? Too much movement, too much noise, too many other children, too many adults, or too many things to see at once can upset or scare infants. In general, avoid (1) large areas of brightly colored, highly figured wallpaper or murals; (2) sharply contrasting colors on walls; (3) too many hanging objects—banners, kites, mobiles, signs—in bright colors; (4) large rooms with many children and teachers. Additionally, individual needs for stimulation, quiet, and order need to be acknowledged and accommodated. Providing a space where infants can feel safe and calm supports their mental as well as physical health.

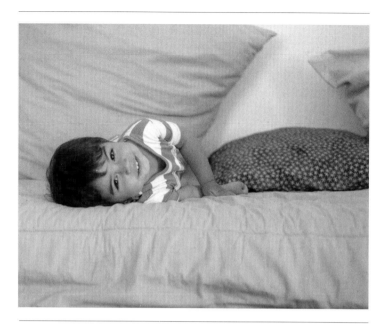

Comfort

A comfortable setting helps you and the infants and toddlers relax and enjoy each other and creates harmony and feelings of peacefulness. An infant needs a place to rest, a place to find a warm shoulder to nestle in, and a low-pile rug to crawl on with ease. A toddler may need a quiet, private space to be alone or to cuddle and hear a story. Both children and adults find different things comforting based on their temperaments and experiences. One child may find comfort in a nook that evokes a sense of privacy, while another might feel more content in the midst of activity. Your environment should have both a quiet place and a active place. Learn through observation how each child responds to different settings and adapt environments accordingly. Think about what makes you feel comfortable, too.

The first step in creating comfort is to make sure that everything is safe and promotes health. Just knowing that the setting is safe and healthy will add to your peace of mind.

Walls, Ceilings, and Floors

To establish a comfortable environment, start with the walls, ceilings, and floors. Here are some ways to add comfort to the permanent environment:

- Use neutral, soft, and natural colors on walls, room dividers, and ceilings.
- Have a mixture of natural light and full-spectrum lighting. Make sure all lights have covers, and no lighting is harsh.
- Provide fresh air as much as possible. Screened windows that open are best.
- Reduce noise by using sound-absorbing materials, such as acoustic ceiling tile, fabrics on walls, and rugs and rug pads on floors, to soften sound.

Furnishings and Materials

Once the fixed elements of the indoor environment are taken care of, you can focus on making the environment more comfortable in the following ways:

- Display pictures and other things that you and the children will enjoy looking at and that will have a calming effect on everyone.
- Furnish the room with soft seats, couches, cushions, and pillows that invite children and adults to curl up and get cozy.
- Provide contact with nature: a garden, small animals, a fish tank, a terrarium, a bird cage, indoor plants, window boxes, flowers. Remember to consider the needs of any person who has allergies.
- Create multilevel surfaces, such as steps, platforms, and lofts, so that you can meet comfortably, eye to eye, with infants and toddlers.

Culturally Sensitive Comfort

Providing comfort for infants, toddlers, and their families includes being responsive to their cultural context. Families are all part of a larger cultural context to which they may be strongly or loosely connected, depending on the individual family's circumstances. The best way to learn about what is important to family members is to establish a relationship with them and to ask questions that will help you to learn about their perspectives and priorities. What is comforting to one person may be uncomfortable to another, so it is important to have discussions.

- Ask family members about the ways they set things up at home to provide care for their child; find ways to include some of those ways in your environment.
- Be sensitive to cultural messages conveyed through the environment in decorations, colors, and furniture. For example, for some families a hammock swing may feel cozy, but for others it may seem unusual.
- Provide different types of comfortable seating, from cushions on the floor to straight-back chairs depending on the people who use the space; be tuned in to physical limitations such as back problems, which may limit a person's ability to be comfortable on the floor.
- Let children show you what they find comfortable and comforting, one child may like to snuggle at naptime with a toy plastic hammer he brought from home, not a typical comfort toy, but his choice will make sense to him and his family.

Convenience

A convenient setting meets the needs of both children and teachers and makes the space workable. You must be able to get what you need easily. Infants and toddlers should be able to see and reach their own play materials. Inconvenient arrangements cause frustrations and unhappiness in children and fatigue and tension in teachers.

Enhancement of Well-being

A convenient environment helps you care for infants and toddlers by making health and safety easier to ensure. When diapering and food preparation areas are planned with convenience in mind, you do not have to leave a child to find something. When areas are arranged conveniently, you are available when needed. Convenience reduces stress on you, which adds to everyone's well-being.

You get maximum health and convenience when settings and activities match. For example, a rug is not easy to clean, so do not put one in the feeding or messy play areas. A rug stays wet and promotes the growth of germs. A washable floor is a better choice for feeding and messy play areas.

You can prevent illness and encourage health by making the practice of healthful habits convenient: (1) organize all areas for quick, easy cleaning; (2) keep supplies and cleaning equipment nearby but out of children's reach; and (3) make sure hand-washing facilities are convenient for children and adults.

Order and Accessibility

When materials are set out in a convenient way, volunteers, family members, and part-time helpers can come in and work more easily. They can find what they need right away. When materials are stored in a logical manner that makes them easily accessible, other adults can also help put things away without having to ask you where to put them because everyone can see where the objects belong.

A well-ordered and convenient setting makes activities more predictable because the teacher and the children know where to get the items they need throughout the day. For example, in one classroom a teacher decided to move the trash can, and the toddlers in her small group continued to throw their paper towels and cups where the trash can used to be. They were accustomed to the predictable location of the trash can, and the change was confusing. Predictability means you know what to expect. Children learn what to expect. A well-organized setting facilitates finding things. Children know where to go when they want or need something. A predictable environment helps everyone feel secure.

To create order and accessibility:

- Put play materials within the children's reach on open shelves.
- Have enough accessible storage places for extra toys and supplies.
- Keep all items organized; assign each toy or material to its own storage place.
- Have comfortable places for teachers to sit at the children's level.
- If a family member uses a wheelchair, would he or she be able to enter the areas where other family members visit?
- Use an open-center arrangement for ease of movement, with large perma-

nent equipment around the perimeter of the room.
- Locate diapers and the changing table within easy reach for you but out of reach of infants and toddlers.
- Use simple, portable barriers to keep toddlers from hurting crawlers or young infants and to keep crawlers from interfering with toddlers' games.
- Create separate activity areas for the children, but maintain an open view for teachers.

An Enriched Program

Convenience means designing your environment so that movement and placement of equipment make the day easy for you and the children. Convenience means having the right things in the right places. It also means having plenty of well-organized storage space, handy shelving, cubbies, and materials. These kinds of arrangements free up valuable time and allow you to provide more choices of activities to the children.

Child Size

An environment that fits one's size feels right. A place that does not may feel uncomfortable. Adults feel out of place sitting in tiny chairs at elementary schools on back-to-school nights. Young children may well feel out of place in a room with only adult-sized furnishings. Unless children have child-sized equipment, they may feel as though they live in a world of giants.

Furnishings and Equipment

Child-sized chairs, tables, shelves, sinks, toilets, and climbing structures help toddlers play, reach materials, and move things. As mixed-age groups become more prevalent, teachers can help each other find ways to balance out the changing needs, abilities, interests, and sizes of the children in their care. Infants and toddlers need to be able to reach playthings safely without climbing or stacking furniture.

For example:

- Tables should meet the following standards to fit children based on their sizes:

  – 12 inches high for children six to fifteen months of age
  – 14 inches high for children twelve to twenty-four months of age
  – 16 inches high for children eighteen to thirty-six months of age

- Children's feet should be planted on the floor when they sit in a chair. Recommended heights of chairs or stools are:

  – 5.5 inches high for children six to fifteen months of age
  – 6.5 inches high for children twelve to twenty-four months of age
  – 8 inches high for children eighteen to thirty-six months of age

- Slides for children under eighteen months of age should be 24 inches or less, for children eighteen to thirty-six months, no higher than 3 feet.
- Easels for toddlers should be 10 to 14 inches off the ground, depending on age. Tabletop easels can be used on a table or even on the floor for children with special needs who are not able to stand while painting on an easel.
- Child-sized steps should be 4 to 5 inches high and 10 to 12 inches deep to accommodate a crawling child.
- Toys should be within reach on low shelves, less than 24 inches high.
- Riding toys should be easy to move and easy for children to get on and off.
- Child-sized toilets at a height of 12 inches encourage self-care.
- Hand-washing sinks should be the following heights:

  – 16–18 inches high for children under twenty-four months
  – 21–22 inches high for children eighteen to thirty-six months of age

- Allow for specialized accommodations when including a child with a disability or other special need. For example, if a child is interested in the loft but is unable to navigate the entry, an adult should be able to maneuver comfortably to place a child into the loft.

Space and Equipment

Flexibility helps you maintain a truly interesting environment for infants and toddlers. To be able to change the space easily, you need lightweight, easy-to-clean equipment so teachers can move things about without strain. Ways to create flexibility include:

- Using easy-to-move equipment
- Keeping the center of the room open for different uses throughout the day or week
- Having different kinds of toys and equipment within easy reach
- Using foam cushions or bolsters as barriers or fences
- Using an empty plastic wading pool for young infants' play
- Using a pile of pillows to separate groups or activities
- Using modular boxes, blocks, or risers (4 to 12 inches high) to create instant room dividers or playhouses
- Using an area for more than one purpose: the feeding area for messy or water play, the couch for one-to-one interaction or storytelling

Movement

Movement is essential to growth, allowing young children to practice their physical skills and develop their ability to think; movement provides information about the world. For example, if an environment has shallow carpeted steps to climb on, infants can safely learn lessons about gravity.

Flexibility

The environment should offer many choices: for movement, quiet play, rest, messy activities, privacy, a chance to be with other children, and a place for a teacher and one child to be together. Offering all this under one roof requires flexibility—the ability to make changes easily and to use some areas for more than one purpose. The environment needs to:

- Meet the needs of both the youngest infant and the oldest toddler in your group.
- Offer choices suited to the preferences of different children.
- Meet each child's daily needs for vigorous play, quiet rest, privacy, cuddling, and time with playmates.
- Be adaptable to the changing needs and abilities of children as they grow.

In an environment that is safe for movement, you can let infants explore on their own. Their ability to do so tells the infants they can be somewhat independent but still secure. And because the infants can move about and make choices according to their developing abilities, teachers can observe and work with individual children. If a child has a disability or other special needs that impact physical movement, experiencing exploration through movement is still important. The child's family members and specialists can demonstrate ways of moving the child's body through space and, if appropriate, equipment such as a scooter board or other wheeled device.

You can ensure safe movement by providing:

- Clean floor surfaces that are not slippery
- Fenced and groomed outdoor play areas
- Appropriate support or facilitation for a child with disabilities or other special needs
- Durable and secure climbing structures built over recommended shock-absorbing surfaces

Do not use walkers, swings, or jump seats. They limit natural movement and encourage accidents (therapeutic walkers used by children with physical disabilities are appropriate if recommended). Toddlers will move whether moving is safe or not. They constantly try out new movement skills and explore their independence. A well-designed environment encourages and allows safe exploration while giving toddlers the feeling of testing their limits. At the same time, the setting must be free of really dangerous challenges and discourage unsafe explorations. *The idea is to let toddlers do what they need to do and to enable them to do it safely.* For example, toddlers need to:

- Climb—where the ground is padded
- Run full speed—down a carpeted hallway
- Jump—and land on a mat

Arrangement of Space and Equipment

To encourage infants and toddlers to move freely, provide plenty of supervision and:

- Protected areas for young infants to stretch and move safely
- Safe open spaces to crawl
- Multilevel environments—lofts, ramps, pits
- Surfaces with many different textures
- Floors that are not slippery
- Clear, open pathways
- Nearby outdoor play areas
- Steps or ladders and ramps for climbing
- Large-muscle equipment—tunnels, slides, mattresses, hanging bars, rocking boats, balance beams, hammocks, risers, pillow piles, tumbling mat, playpit

Arrange the furniture and large equipment to encourage safe, free movement. Watch for anything that limits movement. Young children need to be able to lie on their backs, roll, sway, crawl, sit, bounce, run, climb, jump, grasp, bend, turn, stamp, and march. You need to know the children are safe while they are doing so. Your environment should both encourage such activities and allow for easy supervision.

Choice

As a teacher, you will want to offer plenty of choices. An environment with numerous textures, activities, and equipment provides infants and toddlers many appropriate choices—which also helps you. Letting young children choose their own activities reduces a teacher's stress. An environment with a good mix of developmentally appropriate activities lets infant care teachers learn, too. This kind of environment frees you to observe and respond to the children. By watching, you can see what attracts each child, observe a child's skill level, notice what each child finds challenging, and learn how to better prepare the environment for future learning. Letting children choose makes it easier for you to do a good job.

Range of Choices

The setting should offer a range of developmentally appropriate choices that support growth. Children who can choose what is interesting to them will pick what meets their needs. Self-selection allows children to feel that what they want to do is acceptable to adults. You can ensure rich, developmentally appropriate choices in the following ways:

- Set up areas for different types of activities: large motor, small motor, sensory perception, creative expression.
- Cover the floor with a variety of textures so that various kinds of activities can easily take place in different areas. Diverse floor surfaces will prompt you to provide a range of choices.
- Provide opportunities for privacy so that children have the choice of being alone or in a small group. Create areas where children feel a sense of privacy but where you can still see them to supervise.

- Keep the center of the room free so the children can see the play options around the perimeter.
- Arrange low shelves so that toys have space around them, and children can focus on each choice.
- Use safe outdoor space for a range of experiences, not just large-muscle activities. Provide sights, smells, textures, water play, and areas for activities such as telling stories or singing songs.
- Offer a variety of playthings and materials, and change what you offer from time to time.
- Make opportunities for water play available daily.
- Provide frequent opportunities for messy play.

In sum, whether a family child care home or a child care center, whether you are designing a new environment or rearranging your current one, use the eight key concepts as your guide. Try to get in the habit of considering these concepts each time you contemplate a change. Ask yourself how your environment will best (1) ensure safety, (2) promote health, (3) provide comfort, (4) be convenient, (5) be child-sized, (6) maximize flexibility, (7) encourage movement, and (8) allow for choice while being accessible and culturally welcoming for all children.

Section Two:
Planning Your Infant/Toddler Care Setting

No single plan can show you exactly how to set up an ideal space for your child care needs; too much depends on the particulars of your program. In any setting, the environment plays a pivotal role in the quality of services the program provides to infants, toddlers, and their family members. Whether you are designing a new environment or making changes to an existing program, the process involves planning, design, money, and effective management. Obtaining the services of a professional who has experience in designing early childhood environments will help ensure that you make good decisions the first time and help minimize costly mistakes. While infant care teachers are responsible for implementing changes and troubleshooting issues that arise, the support of the program leader is essential for positive and effective changes to take hold in a program. A family child care provider is often both program leader and infant care teacher and, therefore, is responsible for both planning and implementation.

When a care program is engaged in the design or renovation of a facility, it is important to examine first the design to ensure that the facility will reflect and support the program goals. Group size, room size, age groupings, plumbing (amount, height, placement), indoor-outdoor access *(and the details of the play yard design)* all have an impact on relationships and interactions. For instance, if you want to implement continuity of care, which means that children and teachers are together for the first three years, then a pod design works well (Figure 1). Additionally, all of these elements have an impact on the quality of interactions. When a setting is safe and comfortable, infant care teachers can focus on infants and toddlers and their experiences in the program.

The environmental arrangements made will also depend on whether you are providing care in a permanent child care setting or in a setting used for other purposes. For example, space needed for other purposes on weekends and evenings, such as family living areas in a family child care home or space in churches or multipurpose facilities, have different considerations from programs located in sites used solely for child care.

Your setting will also have fixed features that you cannot easily change. You will need to adapt your environment to these features as well as to other special conditions.

Many program considerations will come into play as you design the environment to fit the unique aspects of your program and setting. For example, if you work in a center with other teachers, your needs will differ from those of a teacher who works alone or from a family child care provider who is adapting a home to care for children. Programmatic issues you must consider include:

- Who will be there—how many children of what ages and age groupings, and how many infant care teachers?
- How much space do you have available?
- How much other space can you use (hallways, other classrooms, outdoor areas, and so on)?
- What are the special features of your environment?
- Can you make permanent changes?
- How will weather affect your use of space?
- What is the purpose of your program?
- In what ways can you make ecologically sound choices?
- How do family members use the environment, and how would you like them to use it?
- What are you trying to accomplish?
- How does the environment help or hinder you?
- How many hours a day will children be with you?
- What are the cultural backgrounds of the children and the families served?
- What state and local rules and regulations do you need to learn about before you make changes to your environment?

Before you arrange your environment, look at it from the perspective of an infant or toddler. See how the setting works for the small child by getting down and moving as an infant does. Think about how

a crawling child would navigate. Think about older infants and how they move and interact. Consider the unique aspects of your program, particularly the ages of the children and the characteristics of the setting in which you provide care.

Think about your own needs as well. How can you arrange and adapt the environment so that you can conveniently get to necessary supplies, sit comfortably with children for meals, and have easy access to documentation materials when you need them? When daily routines are supported by a well-planned and carefully organized environment, you can enjoy your time with the infants and toddlers more easily.

Environments and Different Age Groups

When you are setting up a caregiving environment, one of the most important issues to consider is the children's ages. Infancy is generally described as the period from birth through twenty-four to thirty-six months. Obviously, there are many differences in the needs and abilities of children in that age range. The PITC DVD *The Ages of Infancy: Caring for Young, Mobile, and Older Infants* (1990) presents more information on this topic.

You need to consider six issues related to age when you are setting up environments for infants and toddlers:

1. Are you going to serve groups of children of about the same age or children of mixed ages?
2. If the children are about the same age (young, mobile, or older), what needs does that specific age group have?
3. If you are setting up mixed-age groups, how can you support the optimal development of each child in the group, including a child with disabilities or other special needs?

4. How will you design your environment to meet those needs?
5. How will you be able to alter the environment as the children grow older or as you bring in younger children?
6. What resources do you have to help you consider how the environment can support a child with disabilities or other special needs?

Young Infants (Birth to Six or Eight Months)

The young infant who is not yet crawling needs to feel secure in the environment and to trust the people who are caring for him or her. When you are setting up environments to serve very young infants, remember the following:

- Small numbers of children and adults are recommended.
- Diapering, feeding, sleeping, and play areas should be set up to allow quiet, personal contact between the infant care teacher and young infant.
- Young infants benefit from being taken to interesting parts of the environment or having things brought to them.
- Young infants like to be held.
- Young infants need to be protected from being hurt by mobile and older infants while still being allowed the freedom to move their bodies.
- The environment should facilitate close physical contact between the infant care teacher and child.
- Watching, listening, and exploring with the body, hands, and mouth are prominent learning activities of young infants.
- Infants spend a great deal of time looking up toward ceilings, walls, and lights.
- Young infants like to practice body movements while they are lying on a firm, cushioned surface.

Mobile Infants (Six or Eight to Fifteen or Eighteen Months)

Infants who can roll, crawl, kneel, sit up, creep, rock, climb up and down ramps and low steps, and cruise (toddle while hanging on to sturdy furniture or railings) fall in this category, as do infants with physical disabilities or differences in the age range who are interested in exploring. Young explorers need an environment that encourages them to use their new skills. The message mobile infants should get from the environment is that it is okay to go after and explore what is there. The message they should get from the infant care teacher is, "I have confidence in your ability to safely explore the environment." When you are setting up environments to serve mobile infants, remember the following:

- Mobile infants are at the peak of sense and motor exploration.
- Infants put almost everything in their mouths.
- Dangerous, breakable, and valuable objects should be kept out of the infants' reach.

match, inspect, and carry things. The older infants rearrange, put in and take out, hide, and discover. They imitate others, play with dolls, paint, draw, smear, take out, hide, and discover. They pour water, sift sand, splash, and make sounds. Older infants use words and understand directions. They can help themselves by washing, eating, and dressing themselves to some degree. When a child has a disability or other special needs that interfere with the development of any of these skills, teachers can learn how to make adaptations to support exploration, discovery, and self-care as appropriate for an individual child.

Environments for older infants must offer variety and opportunities to learn about choice and responsibility. Exploring their individuality is often the central issue

- You need to be able to see the children and get to them quickly. Be available but do not hover.
- Infants with physical disabilities or other special needs may benefit from special assistance in moving and exploring. For example, the child with low muscle tone may be able to move to an area of interest, then need assistance in moving to a stable sitting position for playing. Check with family members and any specialists involved with the family for specific guidance.
- Mobile infants need to be allowed to take small risks.
- Infants do not always have to be close or get in your lap to feel secure. Sometimes a reassuring glance will do.
- Peer play and conflicts begin at this age.

Older Infants (Fifteen or Eighteen to Thirty-six Months)

These youngsters can walk, slide, tumble, climb up, over, and into things, and get up and down stairs. The older infants' small-muscle activities include taking apart, stacking, setting up, and knocking down. The infants keep busy collecting, filling, and dumping. They choose, sort,

• Children like to see their products displayed.
• Children need room and equipment for large-muscle movement.
• Children sometimes do not consider the needs or safety of younger infants in their rough-and-tumble play.
• Older infants need to know the rules for using the environment and the equipment in it.
• Children can use learning centers offering small-muscle activity and sensory perception activities.

If you pay attention to age differences when you set up or change your environment, you will find it easier to meet the needs of all the children you serve, whether in mixed or homogeneous age groups. Another important aspect is how the environmental design supports the program policy of providing each child with close, caring relationships that last over time.

Relationship-based Care

The Program for Infant Toddler Care's (PITC's) six recommended program policies listed here provide guidance for creating a program that is relationship-based. Research and experience show that infant/toddler care and education settings should be organized around the development and maintenance of nurturing relationships between infant care teachers and young children. The design, organization, and use of the environment have a significant effect on the success of these policies. For instance, an environment that offers comfortable seating for a teacher to sit with one or two children (while still being able to visually supervise the rest of the space) supports close connections. The following six policies present an overview of the quality of care an environment can support and protect.

for children of this age. They need teachers who will create an environment that supports creativity, independent action, and curiosity and who will help the infants learn how to share their environment with others.

When you are setting up environments for older infants, remember the following:

• Many children love dress-up and fantasy play. Be sure there are ample props and plenty of space to allow for maximum enjoyment.
• Peer play takes place more and more often. Children who may move more slowly or lack communication skills for entering play may need more adult support to interact with peers.
• It is important for older infants to have ample choices.

Primary Care

In a primary care system, each child is assigned one infant care teacher who is principally responsible for that child's care. When children spend a longer day in care than their primary infant care teacher, a second teacher is assigned to continue primary care for the child. Each child should have a teacher assigned to him or her at all times during the child care day. Teaming is also important. Primary care works best when infant care teachers team up and support each other and provide a back-up base for security for each other's primary care children. Primary care does not mean exclusive care. It means, however, that all parties know who has primary responsibility for each child.

Small Groups

Every major research study on infant and toddler care has shown that small group size *and* good ratios are key components of quality care. The PITC recommends primary care ratios of 1:3 or 1:4 in groups of six to twelve children, depending on the age. The guiding principle is, The younger the child, the smaller the group. Small groups facilitate the provision of personalized care that infants and toddlers need, supporting peaceful exchanges, freedom and safety to move and explore, and the development of intimate relationships. Small groups should have their own environments separate from other groups.

Continuity of Care

Continuity of care is the third key to providing the deep connections that infants and toddlers need in a quality child care program. Programs that incorporate the concept of continuity of care keep primary care teachers and children together throughout the three years of infancy or for the duration of the child's enrollment in care. (See pages 25–26 for an expanded section on continuity of care.)

Inclusion of Children with Special Needs

Inclusion means making the benefits of high-quality care available to all infants through appropriate accommodation and support in order for the child to have optimal active program participation. Approaches already embraced by the PITC—such as care that is based on relationship, that is individualized, and that is responsive to the child's cues and desire to learn—are equally important for children with disabilities or other special needs. Infants who have responsive, enduring relationships develop emotional security, which gives them the foundation for becoming socially competent and resilient. Infants who have individualized care are allowed to learn and grow in their own way and at their own pace.

Individualized Care

Following children's unique rhythms and styles promotes a child's well-being and a healthy sense of self. It is important not to make a child feel bad about him or herself because of biological rhythms or needs that are different from those of other children. Responding promptly to children's individual needs supports their growing ability to self-regulate, that is, to function independently in personal and social contexts. The program adapts to the child, rather than vice versa, and the children get the message that they are important, that their needs will be met, and that their choices, preferences, and inclinations are respected.

Cultural Continuity

Children develop a sense of who they are and what is important in the context of culture. Traditionally, it has been the child's family and cultural community that have been responsible for the transmission of values, expectations, and ways of doing things, especially during the early years of life. As more children enter child care during the tender years of infancy, questions of their cultural identity and sense of belonging in their own families are raised. Consistency of care between home and child care, always important for the very young, becomes even more so when the infant or toddler is cared for in the context of cultural practices different from those of the child's family. Because of the important role of culture in development, infant care teachers who serve families from diverse backgrounds need to:

- Heighten their understanding of the importance of culture in the lives of infants.
- Develop cultural competencies.

- Acknowledge and respect cultural differences.
- Learn to be open, responsive, and willing to negotiate with families about child-rearing practices.
- In this way, families and teachers, working together, can facilitate the optimal development of each child.

These two floor plans, one for an infant room and another for a toddler room, illustrate a design for relationship-based care. Teachers and children can stay connected visually, aurally, and emotionally throughout the day as the teacher engages in one-to-one personal care with each child. The infant care teacher does not need to leave the room for supplies, and the room contains everything the group will need in a day. The small, cozy spaces provide a setting for intimacy, and the flexible open floor area provides an opportunity for teachers to create play opportunities that

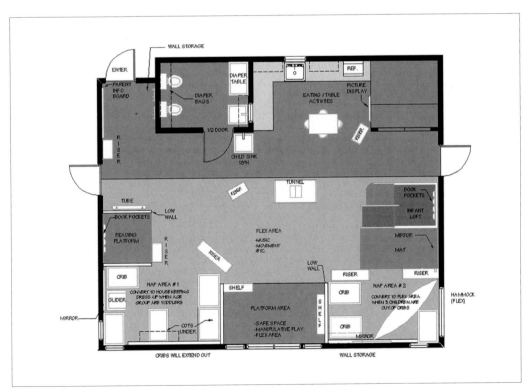

Figure 1. Infant Room

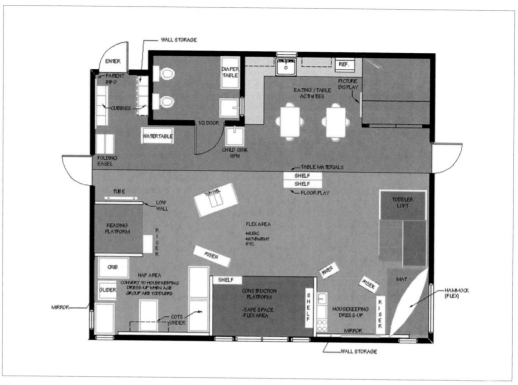

Figure 2. Toddler Room

are directly related to children's emerging interests and abilities.

Environmental Support for Relationship-based Care

Although the six policies noted on page 22 are specifically about relationships, they influence the use of the environment every day. The environment can be designed and arranged to support relationship-based care. Here are some strategies:

- Create close, intimate spaces where a teacher and one or two children can sit together comfortably. Do this outdoors as well as indoors.
- Make sure the teacher can visually supervise the whole room while engaged with one child.
- Pay close attention to the cultural messages you are sending through the environment. Ask staff and family members how they feel about the setting and the décor.
- Provide equipment and furnishings that are movable and adaptable to the different ages of children. For example, the wall climber can be used by a mobile infant who is pulling up to stand and by older infants who can climb up the rungs.
- Design the space with an open center area.
- Create small-group spaces on the periphery of the room for three to four children.
- Provide appropriate environmental adaptations so a child with a disability or other special needs can use the environment as a full member of the group (as adaptations are fairly individualized, seek advice from the child's family members and specialists).

- Use windows as a visual connection to the outdoors.
- Make sure the door is always open to the outdoors, weather permitting.
- Use low walls to separate diaper/toileting areas from the larger room so teachers and children can see each other.
- Divide space by using low walls and see-through plastic barriers to ensure safety, but keep it open visually so the infant care teacher is always visible to the child.

Environmental Design for Continuity of Care

A well-designed environment plays an important role in supporting teachers as they provide continuity of care. Likewise, a disorganized or inconvenient environment can make it much harder for teachers to provide continuous care to children. For instance, if a teacher must leave the room several times a day to take children to a toilet down the hall and be replaced by a "floating" substitute, the connection built between an infant and his primary infant care teacher may be challenged. Implementing continuity of care is made easier by effective environmental design. Many designers and architects of infant/toddler group care settings use what is known as a *pod design* (see Figures 1 and 2). This design provides facilities in the center of a room that can be used by teachers who are each caring for small groups of children. Sinks, toilets, food preparation areas, and supplies are located in the central area. The pod design enables teachers to stay visually connected with children while they are in the central area. The flexible, open area of each room allows teachers to change equipment based on the ages and interests of children in the small group. Programs will still differ in how they offer continuity of care. There are three ways to organize groups to achieve this goal.

Mixed-Age Groups: Expand age ranges to create mixed-age groups, for example, six months to 2.9 years, so that children can remain in the same group as they grow. A child who leaves can be replaced by an infant of the same or different age (similar to many family child care homes). To support a mixed-age group approach, several conditions must be in place:

- The environment must be flexible enough to accommodate young, mobile, and older infants at one time.
- Infant care teachers who work with a mixed-age group need training and knowledge about the different stages of development.
- Children in the group may be divided into close-age primary care groups or mixed-age primary care groups.
- Children who leave the group may be replaced by a child of any age within the age range of the group. However, it may work better for a child of similar developmental level to fill an opening in a mixed-age group of active toddlers. It is not required that the opening be filled by a young infant.
- Different types of room divider systems can be used to protect young infants while allowing them freedom of movement.
- The environment should provide challenges but not overwhelm children. For example, an infant loft has a carpeted slide and wide steps, while the older toddler loft has a taller slide and more narrow and steep steps.

Close-Age Groups That Move: An infant care teacher moves to another setting with children as they grow until they exit the program. The teacher then moves to a new group of infants and stays with them until they leave for preschool. To support a close-age group approach, keep in mind the following ideas:

- The oldest group of children leaves the program, making room for younger children and their primary infant care teacher to move to the space they occupied.
- When infants move to the next room, they are replaced with a new group of babies.
- Children and adults need time to adjust to a new room.
- Infant care teachers and children should be allowed to move favorite items with them to the new environment.
- New children (or another primary group) are added to the room as children grow older and ratios and group size recommendations change.
- If necessary, one primary group (rather than the whole group) can move to the next room.
- When rooms are different sizes, use the larger rooms to accommodate toddlers.

Close-Age Groups That Remain in the Same Environment: The layout and equipment should be modified as children outgrow the infant environment. In close-age groups, when a child leaves, he or she is replaced by another child from the same age range. Keep in mind the following ideas:

- The environment is modified to adapt to developmental changes of the children.
- Furniture and equipment are changed to fit the children's growing size and activity level.
- Furniture and equipment not currently in use (cribs, indoor climbers, small chairs and tables) are stored or used elsewhere.
- The infant nap room can be converted to a play space for two-year-olds as children grow into the older infant stage.

- Low sinks and toilets are installed in or near every room for toilet learning.
- Children who leave the group are replaced with a child in the same age range.

Figure 3, the floor plan of the Educare Center in Omaha, Nebraska, illustrates a part of a large center built for children from birth to five years old. This design contains the following important features:

- The pod design allows for more than one small group of teachers and children to share the same facilities for toileting, diapering, and food preparation.
- There is an observation room for family members, staff members, and students.
- The window box with raised platform affords infants and toddlers a chance to climb up to a higher level and see the outdoors. A Plexiglas barrier in the center divides small groups.
- The blue center hallway provides a space for vigorous play or other activities during inclement weather.
- Each classroom has direct access to the outdoors.

Family Child Care and Center Care

By their very nature, family child care homes and child care center environments differ. Each type has strengths to draw on when the design of infant/toddler care environments is considered. One common mistake is to try to turn a home into a mini-center. Another mistake, sometimes made by center designers who have been told infant care should be homelike, is to try to duplicate a home in the center. What works best is to use a setting's unique aspects rather than try to imitate another setting. Whether in a center or a home, a child and his or her family members should feel "at home" in the program. What feels homelike depends a lot on

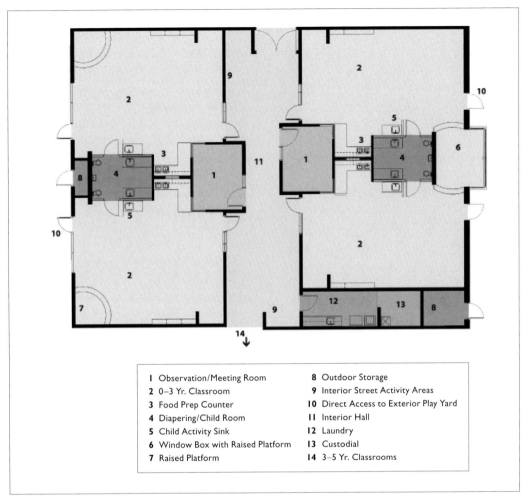

1 Observation/Meeting Room	8 Outdoor Storage
2 0–3 Yr. Classroom	9 Interior Street Activity Areas
3 Food Prep Counter	10 Direct Access to Exterior Play Yard
4 Diapering/Child Room	11 Interior Hall
5 Child Activity Sink	12 Laundry
6 Window Box with Raised Platform	13 Custodial
7 Raised Platform	14 3–5 Yr. Classrooms

Figure 3

a person's experiences. Do not assume that what makes you feel comfortable is the same for others. To learn what makes people feel comfortable, ask them. Engage family members and infant care teachers in dialogues that continue over time about how the program's environment can accommodate people who may have different ideas of what makes an environment welcoming and easy to use.

Family Child Care

The home provides a rich environment with many essentials already in place. Activity areas should clearly differ from one another, and floor surfaces should also vary.

A family child care provider must decide whether to use the whole home environment (either a house or apartment) or to create a child care setting in one or more parts of the dwelling. For instance, a living area may be used as the primary child care setting, and a nearby bedroom is used only for naps. Either choice is workable. Limiting the child care space to one room can mean the space is easier to clean and maintain. Child-sized equipment can be left in place and activity areas established. A disadvantage is that the infants and toddlers miss out on the richness of exploring the variety of environments found in a home and the familiarity and comfort that this experience provides. Some experts suggest using the whole home for just those reasons.

If you decide to use the whole home, a few tips may help. If you have money to spend, put it into basics: install plumbing, such as sinks and toilets, where needed; buy good basic furnishings, low-contrast wallpapers or paints, good storage, carpets, furniture, and outdoor fences. Then improvise. For example:

- Use the couch for large-muscle activity such as climbing.
- Use the kitchen floor for messy play and the bathtub for very messy play.
- Use the coffee table for small-muscle games.
- Take advantage of direct access to the outdoors.
- Throw a sheet over two clotheslines or a table to create a good private play space, inside or outdoors.

Be creative! Observe other high-quality family child care homes and consult children's equipment catalogs for examples of good equipment. Then look around your home. See whether you have things that serve the same function if you use them creatively. Observe how children move and use the space and find ways to support their movements and interests. For instance, many two-year-olds love to push heavy things along the floor; often they choose a child-sized chair or table. You may not feel comfortable with the children pushing chairs or tables around the room, but you could come up with something else that would also satisfy their need to move heavy things around. Some teachers have used milk crates with sand bags inside. Felt pads under the crates protect the floor. The children can gleefully push

the heavy crates to their hearts' content. This is just one example of how to support the children's choices and movements in a way that is appropriate for a particular environment.

If you use your whole home, make sure you remove dangerous and valuable objects, and the house is childproof. Instead of constantly giving infants the message "Don't touch!" you want to be able to give them a nurturing and friendly message: "Come in and share my home with me."

Center Care

Issues of center care include creating intimate settings, small group size, appropriate child-to-staff ratios, and a setting that is soft enough and comfortable enough for infants. Resist the temptation to have your infant/toddler center look like a preschool. Because of their need for close relationships, infants do best in small groups and in close contact with their primary infant care teacher. If you have one large room, divide it into three or four small areas rather than have many infants and teachers together. Ideally, you can do this with real walls and room dividers to minimize noise and help create a feeling of intimacy for the children. Sinks, toilets, diapering, and food preparation areas can be installed in the center of the large room, and small groups can share the use of the facilities. Large groups interfere with the personal relationship between an infant or toddler and his or her primary infant care teacher and with other children. Small groups decrease health and safety risks. Smaller groups can make it easier to promote health by keeping the germ pool smaller. Infant and toddler care works best in groups of six to eight or fewer.

Division and Definition of Space

After you have thought about the unique aspects of your program, you can start designing the environment. Just as your program is unique, so are the special conditions and fixed features of your environment. The amount of space, the quality and quantity of outdoor space, and the location of doors, windows, walls, and plumbing are a few of the many features that differ from setting to setting. That is where environmental design becomes creative. Your task is to create a setting that blends its unique features with the eight key concepts described previously: safety, health, comfort, convenience, child-size, flexibility, movement, and choice.

Deciding how to divide the space to emphasize those key concepts is an important task. You will want to separate messy activities from neat ones, quiet from noisy, and large-muscle from small-muscle activities. You want to set a positive emotional tone. You may find it helpful to consider the following strategies when you define and divide your space:

- Set up activity areas.
- Set up convenient personal care stations.
- Create boundaries and corrals.
- Provide clear, visible order.
- Use the outdoor space all day long.
- Keep the center of the room open.
- Establish many levels.

Activity Areas

Think of activity areas as separate places, like little islands; then work to make them feel separate. You can do that by making sure each activity area has these three qualities:

1. A separate physical location
2. Boundaries that separate it from other areas
3. A mood, feeling, or personality

Arrange the space so different areas are set up for different activities. Each area should have its own function. For exam-
ple, one area is for movement or large-motor activity; another is for quiet rest. This does not mean that children should not move materials around to other areas; indeed, they will because moving things around is important to them. Yet a varied arrangement lets children, who are sometimes energetic and sometimes sleepy, find what they need.

The use of the term *activity* with infants and toddlers indicates what children actually do rather than what teachers might plan. An activity area may invite certain behaviors such as climbing on equipment or sitting at a table for mealtime. But it does not mean that the child will necessarily engage in the way the teacher imagined. For example, a mobile infant may crawl up a ramp and then sit to look at pictures rather than continue climbing around on the equipment. In addition, infants and toddlers often do not make similar choices at the same time, so you may have a child climbing, a child eating, and another sleeping—all at the same time. The picture below shows children playing naptime with a large pillow, ignoring the materials displayed nearby. They are making choices and cooperating with each other.

Some one-room infant/toddler settings have the room completely open, without separate activity areas. This approach usually leads to children clustering around their teacher, moving through the room in a herdlike fashion and not really using toys beyond trying to take things from each other. When the environment is organized into different activity areas, such as a soft area, a large-motor area, an eating area, and a pretend-play area, children tend to occupy different areas of the room according to their varied interests, abilities, and needs. For instance, in a mixed-age setting you may have two toddlers carrying large foam blocks from one corner to another, a mobile infant crawling through a sea of pillows, and a young infant in an enclosed safe space, holding her toes and rolling from side to side. The infant care teacher might be changing a diaper, giving an infant a bottle, or sitting on the floor observing and supporting play. The children are likely to have fewer conflicts. Separate activity areas also encourage children to develop a sense of place. They learn, over time, that it is acceptable to jump, run, climb, and fall in one part of the room but not in the quiet area.

Each activity area should have its own special "feel," making it a mini-environment. Such arrangements prevent boredom and offer sensory variety. Check your activity areas each week, and rotate in new materials, as needed, without changing the area's general purpose. Rotating things keeps activities interesting, though some materials hold children's interest over time and should remain in the setting.

Emotional tone is also important. The feeling of an area should reflect the area's activity. A quiet, restful tone in a large-motor area would be a mistake. Creating a restful feeling in an area where you and one child can curl up together is perfect. Soft colors and furnishings with lots of pillows are welcome in a rest area. Create emotional tone with wall colors, pillows, pictures, banners, hangings, furniture, plants, quilts, wall coverings, and layout. Even when you use color for boundaries, use soft neutral colors such as browns, grays, rusts, ivories, or pastels. These colors can be warm without being too stimulating; children's clothing, playthings, and art can brighten the room. Primary colors are best used only for small items, area outlines, or the moldings. Be aware of how color choices can convey cultural messages. What choices work best for the families in your program?

If young infants are in your group, you can create a small, safe haven inside the playroom just for them. The deck can be open or closed, with a flat or sloping floor and portholes or Plexiglas at the end. This space allows infants to be safe and free to move on the floor without being confined in devices such as swings and bouncy seats that restrict movement and limit choices.

Personal Care Stations

The area where you provide personal care, such as diapering, toileting, washing hands, or changing clothes, should have certain qualities to make it work well. Since it makes sense to have all sinks and toilets near each other on the same plumbing line, the food preparation area will likely be on that line as well. Make sure to follow all recommendations for keeping food and toileting separate from each other! The following features would work well in such an area:

- Barriers such as low walls or half-doors that keep curious children out and safe while allowing teachers continuous visual supervision of the whole room
- Sinks for hand-washing separated from sinks for food preparation
- Counter space for food preparation

- Refrigeration
- Space to store medications out of reach of children
- Convenient storage for diapering, cleaning, and mealtime supplies
- Space for recording observations and daily events

Boundaries and Corrals

Use physical markers to separate activity areas. These boundaries are often walls or doors of rooms, but they can also be seating, storage, developmental barriers (anything that separates children because of their level of development, such as a pile of pillows), and noise absorbers. A corral is a boundary that keeps one age group or activity from another. A portable fence will work as a corral.

You can separate activity areas with physical boundaries such as furniture, shelving, and risers. Consider these qualities when planning boundaries:

1. Height
2. Visibility (Can you see through or over it?)
3. Mass (Can you move it easily?)

A corner requires fewer built boundaries because the walls provide two boundaries. Most boundaries should separate activities without blocking your vision. That means the boundaries should be only as high and as solid as needed to keep a child safe. The teacher needs to see over any dividers into all activity areas. Options for low boundaries include foam beds, mats, area rugs over the carpeting, low risers, and shelving. Boundaries that let children watch others are ideal. Slats, cutouts, or plastic panels can also function as see-through boundaries. They allow infants and toddlers to see you while you care for another child.

Install railings or a handhold for children who are cruising. Leave wide pathways for an unsteady toddler. Arrange the layout so children can see the different areas and get to them easily. Wall and rug color is sometimes used as a boundary and is a simple way to define activity areas. The color tells young children where an activity area begins and ends. When your group includes a child with a disability or other special need impacting independent movement, check that your boundaries do

not interfere with the child's therapeutic walker, wheelchair, or other mobility equipment. For example, area rugs can bunch up when wheels cross over them, yet a child with limited vision may benefit from the dramatic color difference an area rug provides. Adaptations will always depend on the individual child.

Clear, Visible Order

After dividing the room into separate activity areas, make sure the arrangement of materials and equipment is clear and visible to all who use the space. There should be a reason why materials are grouped together. For example, if one of your areas highlights small-muscle activities such as puzzles, bead sorting, tubs and objects to put in and take out, those types of materials should be found consistently in the same area. For your convenience, storage should follow the same order when possible.

An example of creating visible order is the way you put puzzles out for infants and toddlers. Avoid stacking the puzzles. Young children cannot see the ones underneath. For the children's use, put each

puzzle flat on a table, shelf, or floor. Stack puzzles or put them in a rack only when they are being stored.

Another example of how to create clear order is to display dress-up clothes appropriately. Keep them in your creative/expressive activity area. Do not pile them into a box; showcase the clothes. Make them obvious and inviting to the children. Put large plastic hooks on a wooden board mounted on the wall or hang dress-up clothes on a coat rack. Place a picture of each item near the hook: coat, hat, dress, sweater. This arrangement encourages the children to use certain areas for specific activities. It also makes cleanup easier and teaches children about order and how to hang things.

When you set up a clear, visible order, playthings tend to stay in their areas. They do not get scattered, and children learn where play materials belong. Children can eventually help put things away when you give them clear clues.

Outdoor Space

Access to the outdoors is essential for just about everyone. Infants and toddlers enjoy being outside and benefit in many ways. Ideally, children are cared for in rooms that have direct access to the outdoors. In many programs in California, the temperate weather makes it possible to leave doors open for much of the day.

An increased emphasis on natural surroundings in infant/toddler care has led to landscaping and play spaces that make use of trees, hills, pathways, and gardens. Infants need a chance to explore in a safe place outdoors. Do not let being outdoors cause you to use restrictive equipment. A blanket on the grass or an enclosed deck can provide a comfortable space for infants to move their bodies while getting fresh air and enjoying the natural surroundings.

Open Area

No matter what type of setting you have, plan to keep part of it free of hard-to-move equipment. Placing all the large furnishings and equipment along the sides of the room allows you to keep the center open and to alter it as needed. An open center lets the children see what choices are available throughout the room. The children can also get where they want to go easily. They can see the teacher across the room, and the teacher can see and respond to any child who needs attention. An open center creates maximum flexibility and lets children navigate easily between areas.

Define the size of your open center after considering fixed elements, such as windows and doors. Keep the center free of large, heavy equipment or furniture. The space may look empty initially, but you can fill it with many activities each day. A central open space helps you create a rich, varied program.

Multiple Levels

Set up your environment so that infants who are crawling or walking can both see and get to many levels. Use slopes, stairs, or small ladders. Create a pit children can get down into. Different levels provide variety, diverse viewpoints, and numerous chances for movement. By creating various levels, you also expand the space. For example, you can place a big chair or playhouse on the floor level, then use a loft over the same floor space for a climbing apparatus with a platform to play on. Children with physical disabilities can use lofts and ramps as well, although an adult may need to assist them in getting into the loft or navigating the ramp. All children appreciate getting a different view of their world. Make sure that steps are an appropriate depth and height for the children who will be using them. For instance, a crawling infant needs a deeper step to accommodate the length of her body. Wide ramps or slides allow more than one child to use the equipment at a time. Multiple levels also provide comfort for teachers to sit or lean as they sit on the floor with infants and toddlers.

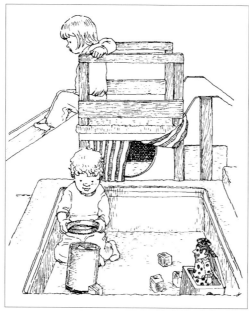

Illustration by Paul Lee

The Big Picture

Each part of the environment has an impact on the children and adults who use the space, so think about the kind of effect you would like each area to have. To make the best use of your resources, think of all the objects in the room as contributing to or detracting from your program's goals, and plan for each object's environmental contribution.

Consider the location of the doors and windows. Design your setting around the fixed features. For example, if you have only one small window 3 feet from the floor, way out of reach of the children, use that source of natural light creatively. Build a loft with its platform right below the window. The children can climb up and look out. Check for any special features such as skylights, built-in room dividers, small alcoves, or changes in floor level. In a small room where space is at a premium, think of what young children need for their growth and development, and make equipment do double duty. A low, carpeted room divider can be a place to sit, something to climb over, a storage area for books or toys, and a hiding place. A table used for snacks or lunch can hold a sand tray or water container for messy play at other times. In cramped quarters, make the maximum use of everything to give the children what they need, and be creative in the use of many levels.

If you have enough space, make sure you do not cram it with too many things. Emphasize large-motor activity and fight the inclination to make little-used space a dumping area.

After you have arranged the room, reevaluate how the children use it. Monitoring is an excellent tool for reevaluation. To monitor simply means to watch what happens. Watch the children in one area or during a particular time, or follow one baby or one teacher for half an hour. Pay attention to the pathways: Are they clear? Does everything seem conveniently arranged? Do you see a lot of frustration? Do children get stuck in a corner that has only one way out? Do they run into each other in a narrow pathway? Another technique is to keep track of how often certain activities take place or how much one piece of equipment gets used. Do children stay in one area or wander freely? Are you finding an increase in conflicts in specific areas? After watching how the children use the environment for a week or two, you may want to change things around. Experiment. Follow your hunches. You can rearrange the layout until you find one that works, but make sure you keep in mind the eight key concepts and the impact the change will have on the children.

Lessons Learned from Others' Mistakes

Whether you are designing a new environment or renovating an older one on a shoestring budget, there is much to be learned from others who have gone before you. Ask colleagues about their experiences with environmental development. When you observe another program that has a feature you would like to incorporate, ask the program leader or teachers how it works for them. Sometimes there are problems that are not immediately visible. A sink might be low enough for toddlers, but the faucet is so far back the children cannot reach it, or a sink is so low that it does not drain properly and actually fills with water when the higher sink drains. One program that provided family services as well as child care found that it helped to have the family services offices near the child care rooms rather than on the other side of the building. Many lofts have been built where the steps are too deep, steep, or high for infants or toddlers. Rather than re-creating mistakes of others, gather information before making expensive changes that you might regret later. Professional designers with a focus on early childhood settings can provide invaluable guidance in this area.

Section Three:
Setting Up Specific Areas

The key concepts and special concerns presented in the previous sections provide guidelines for environmental planning. Apply these guidelines to the specific areas you want to create to achieve an environment that meets the needs of children and adults. Consider the following areas when setting up your infant/toddler environment: entrance and family communication area; areas for learning and development; peer play; multilevel equipment; rest and sleeping; diapering and toileting, washing up, feeding, and food preparation; storage and shelves; and outdoor space.

Remember to include spaces for your own use, such as a place to store personal belongings and a shelf for keeping notes handy for recording observations. You know your environment and your own needs best. When you plan physical space for your notepad, camera, or other documentation tools, it is more likely that you will make a quick note or snap a photo in the middle of the daily activity. It may work for you to have one place in the food preparation area and another shelf outdoors for storing your documentation tools.

In planning different areas, remember that infants and toddlers are explorers, and they will use all areas as they see fit. They will naturally want to move materials from one space to another as soon as they are physically able to do so. Designing specific areas allows you as the teacher to create a sense of order and purpose. However, with the possible exception of keeping messy play in an area you can easily clean, "activity areas" for infants and toddlers are not meant to limit children's movements or use of toys and equipment. For instance, toddlers may take blocks to the fantasy area and pretend the blocks are groceries, babies, or even birthday gifts. An eight-month-old may take a stacking ring and crawl around the room with it. Improvisation should be encouraged and enjoyed.

Entrance and Family Communication Area

A well-defined entrance creates a good place for family members to drop off their infants and toddlers without having to walk across the entire room. The entrance also sets a mood. An attractive and cheerful entrance communicates to the children that they are welcome to enter a special place set up for them. Make sure that you are sensitive to the cultural and ethnic backgrounds of the people in your program and your community when designing the entry area; artwork, furnishings, and color can convey cultural messages. Find out what matters to the families and staff members in your program. For instance, holiday decorations can feel warm and welcoming to some while making others feel excluded.

The entrance to the center should be clearly defined. Entrance activities take place close to the doorway. How the area is arranged is important. The entrance often becomes cluttered or is ignored. It should have a place for the children's belongings, a sign-in sheet, and an area where information for family members can be posted. This area gives the first and last environmental messages to infants, toddlers, and family members each day.

Some centers provide individual cubbies for each infant or toddler; sometimes the cubbies contain a photo of the child or the child's family. A simpler option is to insert large colored plastic hooks in a wooden board placed low enough so children can hang their own jackets. A child's picture and name are displayed above each hook. Shelving can be installed above the hooks for the children's bags and changes of clothing.

The sign-in area, with a place for writing daily reports and family information board, is important. A daily report has space for family members to leave messages such as, "Stayed up late at night." Infant care teachers can also leave messages for family members about the day— what the child ate, bowel movements, or anything special that happened.

A bulletin board near the sign-in area is for family education and communication. Family members can put up notices about babysitting co-ops, classes, social events, garage sales, and family groups. Teachers can post information about public health, infant/toddler development, meetings, and parenting skills. Teachers can also post observations and documentation (including notes, photographs, children's artwork)

that illustrate children's experiences in the program.

If there is room for a couple of chairs or a couch in the area, it can be a place where the child's family and the child's teachers can sit and talk and get to know one another. Consider the ease of getting in and out of the area, especially when multiple families arrive at the same time. When you put energy into making the area welcoming and attractive, the effort will pay off.

Learning and Development Centers

By creating small areas focused on particular activities, you can help infants and toddlers safely experience the world around them.

Small-muscle Activity Areas

Young infants engage in small-muscle activity wherever they happen to be, so a small-muscle activity area is unnecessary for them. Because young infants constantly put things into their mouths, their toys should be large enough to prevent the infants from choking on or swallowing the objects. In a mixed-age group, bringing the very young infant with you to the

The small-muscle area might be placed in an infant corral or on a platform built up with risers of 4-inch steps. Young children can focus better on small-muscle play if the area is clearly defined and no competing or distracting activities are taking place nearby. You can build an instant small-muscle playpit for infants by using large pillows or foam cushions.

For toddlers, small-muscle play means dumping, sorting, and carrying around. The area should contain large plastic interlocking blocks, large beads to string or large pop beads, pegboards, simple puzzles, table blocks, and other small "manipulatives." Infants with disabilities or other special needs may need access to a variety of safe, interactive objects that move or change in sound or sight when the infant does something to them. Commercial toys made for typically developing children can be modified to be even more responsive for children with disabilities or other special needs who cannot easily make toys respond.

You can have low tables in this area or use any low surface for play. Tables are not essential; the floor or a low surface works just as well. Without tables, there is more room to play.

Crayons, play dough, and art activities also offer small-muscle practice. A special favorite of toddlers over eighteen months of age is a chalkboard, which you can make using special green or black paint on well-sanded wood. Put chalkboards at the child's level on the wall, or make them portable and bring them out for use as desired.

Attach a tracking tube onto a wall leading up to the small-muscle area. (The drawing on the next page shows the slanted plastic tube attached to the wall.) A bin underneath holds toys. Two children can play together with the tracking tube: one child places toys in one end; the other

small-muscle activity area for the mobile infants and toddlers allows the different age groups to have contact and interact. Interaction in mixed-age groups requires close supervision to keep infants safe. Objects for small-muscle manipulation can also be brought to the infant one or two at a time, as long as they are not small enough to be a choking hazard.

At about twelve months of age, infants are ready to sort shapes and play with blocks. The infants' play with blocks and other manipulatives will gradually become more sophisticated. The area for small-muscle play is most often carpeted. A carpeted area for dumping reduces noise. Use a low-pile carpet so objects cannot get lost. Nearby shelves and storage are essential because the area can quickly become cluttered if things are not picked up and put away after use.

child waits to pick the toys up at the other end. The tracking tube is also good for solo play.

Sensory Perception Areas

The entire room offers sensory experiences, but you may want to set up one special place for these important learning activities. A corner serves this purpose as the two walls may be covered with carpet samples, pictures, fabric hangings, or quilts. The floor, which may or may not be carpeted, can include many different textures and surfaces. Try to locate the sensory perception area close to a messy play area so that the water tables or tubs are nearby.

Include objects, such as mobiles or wind chimes, in a variety of shapes. Have things that grow or move, such as plants and fish. A terrarium with frogs or turtles is another exciting idea. Use shiny mirrored paper, under protective plastic, for the color and crinkly sound. Use texture boards on the wall or floor for infants. Quilts of various fabrics and textures are also good for infants. They like to see and touch soft sculptures, too.

Some sensory perception activities are temporary arrangements that need close

Illustration by Paul Lee

teacher supervision. Smelling, tasting, and touching different substances for comparison and fun can be done with a few children. The experiences do not have to happen in the more permanent sensory perception areas. Decide which activities you would like to have available daily, and treat those differently from your special sensory perception events.

Pictures, books that offer sensory exploration, and materials to support language development are usually kept in the sensory perception area. Plan some wall space for a bulletin board, which you

can also use for special displays. Put up pictures and shapes, providing toddlers a chance to ask one of their favorite questions: "What's that?" Change the pictures from time to time, and place everything at the child's eye level. Covering pictures with clear contact paper prevents the children from tearing and pulling them.

The environment should have a place for infants and toddlers to look at books, and the books should be available all day. Make the area a special place by using an A-frame book rack to create a wall and make a small reading space. Another option is to have a raised platform in a corner of the room or along a wall. Carpet the platform and add pillows. Use a book holder on the wall to display the books. Toddlers will get practice with motor skills by pulling the books out and learn about organization by putting them back.

The book holder shown below is made from a sturdy canvas fabric with vinyl pockets sewn on to allow children to see the books. The design shown has room for six books. The whole unit gets a lot of wear and tear, so it has to be strong. Have a professional seamstress or tailor make the book holder on an industrial sewing

machine using strong thread. Screw the unit into the wall with a 1-inch by 2-inch piece of wood.

Change the books based on your observations of children's interest in them. Use cardboard books for both infants and toddlers. They cannot turn the pages of cloth books by themselves. However, for very young infants, you may want a supply of cloth books that can withstand pulling and chewing. You will also want books with paper pages that you can read to the toddlers. You may have a shelf up high to store extra books and books that need special care, such as pop-up books, to bring down to read with a child or children during the day.

Large-motor Areas

Design this setting to provide opportunities for young infants to roll over, crawl, and pull themselves up. Mobile infants, especially "cruisers," the children who pull themselves up and hold on to something as they try to walk, need safe areas in which to move about. Toddlers should feel free to walk, run, climb, jump, tumble, and swing. Infants need areas separate from toddlers for maximum safety and freedom for both age groups during large-motor activities. Observe the children in your care, and let them show you what kinds of movements they are interested in. Then adapt the environment accordingly. When toddlers are pushing chairs around the room and laughing gleefully, recognize that this task is developmentally appropriate for them. You may not want them to push chairs, but you can provide crates full of sandbags or something similar so they can follow their urge to push heavy things. For children with delayed motor development, pushing heavy items is often recommended to build muscle tone and provide practice in forward movement. Make the children's natural movements a part of the curriculum, and your days and theirs will be satisfying and fun.

Equipment for developing large-motor skills includes foam or air-filled wedges, seats, tumbling mats, air or water mattresses, low balance beams, carpeted risers (from 3 to 12 inches), adjustable ladders, large balls, tunnels, wheeled toys, beanbag chairs, nets, foam cubes or cushions, hammocks, wagons, swings, riding toys, crates and buckets, barrels, doll strollers, couches, platforms, rocking horses and boats, slides and ramps, bridges, small balls, swivel chairs, rockers, and pillow piles.

Hallways and stairs should be seen as part of the large-muscle area. You can put a barrel tunnel, a pillow hill, or other fun "obstacles" in a hallway. If you have carpeted stairs, make sure there are no loose edges to trip on. Build in a low handrail for beginning walkers.

Use multilevel equipment. An environment with ups and downs gives infants and toddlers good practice, but changes from one level to the next have to be manageable and should lead to something. For example, when stairs lead to a loft platform, the platform may have a special view of the room or more interesting materials for play.

One large-muscle activity option is to create an adventure room containing climbing bars and platforms with railings. The equipment can be set up so a child can jump off one level onto a mat or big foam mattress. The spacing between rungs can let two-year-olds pull themselves to the first level. A horizontal net challenges and delights most toddlers. It is similar to a hammock but strung up much more tightly so there is tension between all four corners; it should only be a few inches above a padded floor or grassy area. Toddlers can climb along it, step through it, or roll around on it and feel it bounce a bit. The net could be attached using sturdy loops, so it can be detached and removed by the teacher. This way the space it fills can be adapted to other uses as well.

Another activity employs plastic milk crates, plastic cube chairs, or strong hollow blocks with small sanded planks. These materials are cheap and can be stored when not in use. Toddlers can create their own structure and crawl under or walk on it. You can use the same materials to build a follow-the-leader course or to make a "loft" using milk crates and a piece of sanded plywood. Put a mattress on top for softness.

Provide walking routes for cruisers. The back or front of a couch makes a good handhold. You can also buy a stair railing and attach it to a wall about 15 inches from the floor. Make sure the railing is splinter-free. Walking routes for cruisers need to be easy to navigate; low-pile carpet works well. Remember to consider these "in-between" children when you design the layout of the room and allow a space for them.

Climbing is important to toddlers. It supports their need to feel independent, gives them a sense of mastery, and helps them figure out how space is arranged. Toddlers will climb no matter what, on a table if nothing else is around. So when you are planning an environment, ask yourself: What is here for toddlers to climb? The dowel climber below is built on a wall and has a 1/8-inch or 1/4-inch Plexiglas mirror behind it, which lets toddlers see themselves climb. The climber is 4 feet wide and 5 feet high. Dowels are set 8 inches apart. The bar that holds the dowels in the middle also divides the climber in two, allowing two children to go up at the same time. The entire climber is made with 2-inch by 4-inch hardwood and 1¼-inch dowels. The climber extends only 4 inches from the wall.

You can connect a detachable slide to a climbing loft or build a slide into a series of risers so there is no place to fall. A double slide provides a great chance for shared fun. Children can go down holding hands or just looking at each other. Often, one child will go up one side while another goes down the other. The area at the bottom of the slide must be kept clear; place a mat or soft carpet there to cushion any falls. Toddlers will go up the slide from the bottom, come down on their bellies, and in general try anything. Slides for toddlers from eighteen to thirty-six months of age can be 3 feet high. For children less than eighteen months old, slides should be a maximum of 24 inches high.

> *Slides for toddlers from eighteen to thirty-six months of age can be 3 feet high. For children less than eighteen months old, slides should be a maximum of 24 inches high.*

A loft platform 26 inches high with an opening at one end can be used by toddlers for jumping onto a futon or air mattress placed below. At other times, the opening of the loft can be enclosed by a gate that serves as part of a railing.

A free corner is a good place to cover the floor with an air mattress, gym mats, a futon mattress, or foam mats placed side by side. Line the walls up to 2 feet high with carpet samples to soften them, too. Toddlers can jump up and down in this area.

Creative Expression Areas

The area that fosters fantasy play and peer socialization the most is the creative expression area. Tables scaled to size, about 10 inches high, where two or three children can work together, are ideal for play with crayons or play dough. Infants and toddlers can sit, kneel, or squat at that height, using their whole bodies while they work.

A wall easel built for two is helpful. For children eighteen to thirty-six months of age, painting is a motor activity. Toddlers use their bodies to paint, so they need plenty of elbow room. Mount a piece of plywood sideways; the size will depend on the amount of space available. Seal the board with semigloss paint and two coats of polyurethane to make it washable. You can build a paint tray onto the board at 10 to 14 inches from the floor. You can also use the wall itself as an easel. Paint the easel area a light color, and add a paint tray.

Display the children's artwork on bulletin boards that are low enough for the children to see. The display gives children a chance to point to their work and talk about it.

Many expressive materials are messy, requiring special setups. The most important messy play uses water. Research indicates that regular water play reduces stress. Water is soothing; infants can watch its movements, hear the sounds it makes, and feel its temperature. Toddlers can pour water and use it for bathing dolls and washing dishes or cars.

A water table (a table with sides that can hold water or other things) is ideal for children two years old or older. The table should be between 18 and 24 inches high, depending on the age of the children, and placed on an uncarpeted, skidproof floor, preferably near a sink or in the kitchen. You can offer variety by making the water soapy, cold, colored, or warm. Have storage nearby for appropriate playthings: measuring cups and spoons, ladles, spoons, plastic containers, funnels, sifters, sieves, and sponges. Fill the table with other substances besides water sometimes: beans, sand, gelatin, rice, shredded paper, grass, oatmeal, large rocks, cornmeal, paint, or clay. A tray with a thin layer of sand and some small dump trucks and diggers can be a wonderful opportunity for creative and cooperative play.

Dishwashing tubs or large plastic trays can work as water tables or sand trays.

Put them on a steady table over linoleum flooring, not carpeting. Use small wading pools for infant play; fill it with leaves or balls, or something else that could be fun and safe to explore. Make sure to find a wading pool that is safe for infants to climb in and out of without tipping over. Many family child care homes use the bathtub for finger painting and other messy activities. Remember that children in diapers should not sit in water with other children.

Troughs built around a faucet at ground level allow for further play in the water. Make the sides 6 to 12 inches high, and place the troughs on a floor surface that is easy to mop. Keep children under constant supervision during water play, and empty the trough when they are finished playing.

Peer Play Areas

Peer play will occur throughout the environment, particularly among older infants, but there are specific ways to encourage interaction. Although setting aside a specific area for peer play is not necessary, certain environmental arrangements should be made throughout the setting to encourage peer play.

Researchers have found that fixed equipment, such as climbers and slides, stimulates cooperative peer play, as do hallways and stairs. Toys and planned activities do not work as well.

A narrow slide can lead to trouble because toddlers often fight over who goes first, but a wide or double slide fosters peer play. Infants less than eighteen months of age usually prefer a single slide

with handrails on each side. Toddlers do well on a wide slide. An alternative that works for both infants and toddlers is to have double slides, two slides side by side. Leave 2 inches between the slides so no fingers can get caught.

Make all passages wide enough for two children, at least 30 inches; passages include the stairs up to the loft platform, a walking ramp, slides, the climbing equipment, and the stairway landing. You can also arrange furniture to support peer activities. For example, a round table with two or three chairs encourages peer table work. When arranged for dressing up, the semi-enclosed area under a loft can be just right for dramatic play. The loft platform itself can easily be occupied by two or three toddlers.

Dramatic-play areas always stimulate peer play. Older infants set out dishes, pretend to wash them, or serve pretend food. Include in this area numerous household items for children to handle and carry around, using real things whenever possible. You can often get good secondhand plastic plates, metal tableware, and sturdy pots and pans at thrift stores or garage sales. Spools 16 inches high from electric companies make good low tables for two or three toddlers. Other items for dramatic play include telephones, dress-up clothes, mirrors, mops, brooms, purses, suitcases, dolls, boxes, doll furniture, and stuffed animals.

A tunnel is great for social play. It must be wide enough for two toddlers to sit inside comfortably. The middle can have a place, also big enough for two, for children to stand up and look about. Build portholes along the sides to allow children to peek in or out. Make an instant tunnel from a sono tube—a large tube made of stiff cardboard. Used for pouring concrete, sono tubes come in different sizes up to 4 feet wide. Check with a construction company for availability. Also explore industrial areas of town for leftover materials that you could turn into playthings. Make sure all materials are safe and nontoxic.

Mirrors also encourage peer relations. Use Plexiglas mirrors, which you can order from a large plastics company. Make sure the mirrors are full length and wide enough so that two or three infants or toddlers at a time can sit or stand in front of them. Try to put a mirror near the dress-up clothes.

Rocking boats can help young children learn how to cooperate. Rocking boats also enable two children to have fun moving together. Often, climbing in and out of the rocking boat is an important part of the play. A double hammock made of cloth is another place in which two toddlers can swing or relax together.

Set up sturdy plastic or inflatable wading pools without water. Add blankets and dolls to create a small, safe play area for

two or three infants. This arrangement gives infants a quiet place to focus on their play. If you put the pool near a chair or couch, you can sit nearby and hold one child while others are playing.

Add curtains here and there to create places for children to play peek-a-boo; for example, hang a curtain from the overhead loft into the play area. Cutouts, or portholes, in tunnels or loft fences also make good peek-a-boo places. Infant care teachers can also use small pillows, books, or pieces of cloth for peek-a-boo games with infants. Some teachers have used sheer scarves or see-through fabric in front of small spaces that children can fit into, such as between the side of a shelf and the wall, giving the child the feeling of privacy while allowing the teacher to keep an eye on the child.

Multilevel Areas

Options to create a multilevel environment include lofts, raised platforms, playpits, movable risers, and furniture, such as chairs and couches.

Lofts

Lofts, which can include platforms, stairs, ramps, slides, tunnels, and suspension bridges, may be used for privacy, small group activities, and large-motor practice. The loft platform does not need to be higher than 36 inches, the height of a tall toddler. At this height, you can relate to a child easily and can look the child in the eye. Use see-through loft boundaries so the child does not feel caged. Make railings from wooden slats or Plexiglas panels. Wooden slats should be vertical, as horizontal slats can be used as a ladder. If the loft is more than 36 inches high, make sure it is safe. Get a detachable slide for the loft. Build locked storage underneath for the slide and other materials.

Use the space under the loft for a dramatic-play area or quiet play spot. Put mirrors, shiny mirrored paper, mobiles, pictures, or textures on the ceiling (the underside of the loft). A low table in the area gives young children a raised surface for play. Small shelves underneath and on the loft provide storage.

Even a small room can accommodate a loft at one end. The loft can be as small as 4 feet wide and 4 feet deep. Stairs in the middle and a platform on either side create four separate areas.

Raised Platforms

Small raised platforms create spaces for special activities. In a small room, you can have one raised platform for working with blocks and another for books. Raised platforms keep similar activities and their materials in one area.

A reading platform built into a corner or against a wall can be as small as 4 feet by 3½ feet. Make the platform about 4 inches high, carpet it, and add pillows for comfort.

You can build a raised platform with 2-inch by 4-inch wood boards and ¾-inch plywood. Cover the platform with low-pile carpeting in a neutral color. For a block

area, do not put any padding other than carpeting on the platform because building with blocks requires a firm surface. The blocks should be stored on an adjoining shelf. Put a container of toy cars on the shelf, too.

Create a general-use raised platform with as many as three 12-inch deep, 4-inch high carpeted steps leading up to it. Make the first step a movable riser. (See Movable Risers below for suggestions on use.) The raised platform is an ideal space for young infants less than fourteen months old; they can crawl up the steps, lie on them to play with toys, and crawl to the top and roll down without hurting themselves. Older infants and toddlers need more challenges. For those children, you can make the steps 8 inches deep.

Playpits

Playpits can be built into lofts, raised platforms, or the floor of the room. The playpits provide a safe haven for infants, a defined space for play, and a sensory experience when filled with rubber balls or other soft objects.

Movable Risers

Use carpeted risers of various heights to create different levels. Two risers placed at right angles in a corner create a playpit. The first step of a platform can be placed on top of the second step (which is then 8 inches high) to make a cruising bar.

Toddlers love to jump off risers and use them as balance beams. Risers can also be used to separate activity areas.

Furniture

A couch or overstuffed chair can become a second level. Use a portable ramp or slide; make sure to anchor it safely. You can also put a small portable staircase with two or three steps next to the couch or chair. A mobile infant or toddler can use

sleeping area apart from the noisy space. When staff members are available to monitor the children, the best arrangement is to have a separate room for sleeping.

Rest Areas

The children will not all get tired at the same time, and some will want to take only a short break but not sleep. Children like to relax and rest even when they do not feel like sleeping. Be sensitive to when individual infants and toddlers need rest and provide for it. Some children do not give clear signals when they have had enough stimulation. Ask family members how they know when their child needs a break. Children have very different tolerance levels for activity. Doing something that seems ordinary for a child who is typically developing may be fatiguing for children with physical differences or health issues. Just being around other people may fatigue some infants or

the staircase to climb up to the arm of the furniture.

Rest and Sleeping Areas

Infants and toddlers in child care should be able to rest or sleep when they are tired. An infant who wakes up often during the night may need more sleep the following day. A toddler just getting over a cold may need two naps instead of the usual one. The environment should have places where children can relax and a place where they can take a nap with their own bedding whenever they are sleepy.

Rest and sleep should be planned for in different ways. Infants and toddlers often rest by playing quietly or just lying down and gazing. Rest does not require as much protection as sleep. A young child can rest while he or she looks at a book or watches others play quietly. Sleep requires a secluded spot away from noise, movement, and stimulation. Set the

not sit there. If you do not sit there, the children cannot crawl onto your lap when they need to.

Set up quiet places on the edge of the playroom for resting. These places may be window seats, small carpeted platforms, soft enclosed areas—even flat stair landings or a pile of cushions collected in a quiet spot will work. Adding pillows, blankets, and soft toys to a carpeted platform can make it an ideal resting place. Pillows and cushions help screen out noise and other stimulation. Keep the colors of the pillows neutral and soft; avoid bright colors. Everything about a quiet spot should be restful.

A place to be alone. You can set up small private areas around the room. A second option is to put a canopy or small parachute over a loft to create a tent-like space. Lace curtains under a loft can provide a sense of privacy for a child while a teacher can still see through the lace to visually supervise the child. Make sure to check with your local fire marshal about rules regarding hanging fabrics; the rules vary in different areas.

Hammocks make good private spaces and are cozy places to cuddle with a teacher. Although they swing, hammocks are safer than rockers. Hammocks can hold infants or toddlers and feel comforting. Also, hammocks can be put up or taken down easily, thus saving space. A double width, all-cloth hammock is the best.

Use of the couch. A hypoallergenic couch can provide comfort for both infants and teachers. Two teachers can sit on a couch with one or two children each. Choose a couch for teacher comfort, and add pillows to make infants and toddlers cozy.

The couch can be used for resting, climbing, or as a walking rail for cruisers. Make sure the cover fabric is soft and easy to clean. Avoid stimulating colors and patterns. A removable, washable cotton

toddlers. So it is helpful if the environment has rest areas that are always available.

Good resting places include armchairs, rocking chairs, playpits, quiet decks or lofts, carpeted barrels, couches, pillows, low mattresses, and hammocks. Foam chairs or couches that open into mats take up little space. Be sure the adult-sized furniture is comfortable and provides good spinal support for teachers. If a couch or chair does not feel good to you, you will slipcover is a good choice for covering a couch. Another low-cost option is a fabric "throw," a large square of material that can be draped over the couch. Fabric throws with foam backing will stay in place as you and the children use the couch. A throw is easy to take off, wash, and put back on. The couch is like a welcoming grandparent. It provides an ideal place for infants, toddlers, and teachers to relax.

Sleeping Areas

The napping space must feel safe and secure. It should be peaceful like the bedroom in a home. Of course, there are differences; putting infants to sleep on adult beds, couches, or waterbeds is not safe. Napping places must be far away from areas where large-motor activities take place and preferably traffic is limited. The area should also be shaded and well ventilated. Use a dimmer switch on the lights, and turn the lights down low or off. The fewer sleepers in an area, the fewer interruptions in sleep there will be. Include some plants and soundless hanging mobiles in the area for the children to look at. In some cases, you might use a radio or white-noise machine to mask traffic, construction, or other significant noises that interfere with sleep.

Scale the furnishings to the size of the children. Have mats, cots, or cribs that will feel cozy and comfortable. Using a firm, fitting mattress in a sturdy crib in which all pillows, fluffy quilts, comforters, sheepskin, stuffed toys, and other soft products are removed reduces risk factors for sudden infant death syndrome (SIDS) in young infants under eight months old. Each infant and toddler should have his or her own spot to sleep. Port-a-cribs save space but are not very sturdy. Cots made to stack and store or mats work well for toddlers. When covered with a blanket, the cots are comfortable.

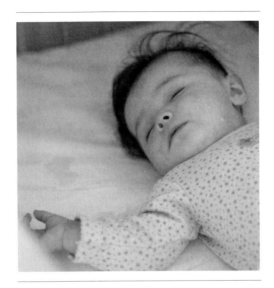

If the sleeping area is part of a large room, set it off from activity areas with a divider that is at least 4 feet high. When permitted by fire codes, you might use fabric banners hung from the ceiling to act as soft walls. A corner works best because you already have two walls. Use lots of fabrics—cushions, pillows, blankets, quilts—to absorb sound. Put up wall hangings, but keep colors and patterns neutral and low key.

Storage for bedding has to be accessible to you but out of the children's reach. The best storage has compartments, each labeled with a child's name and big enough for the child's blanket, favorite toy, and sheet.

When you have finished designing your rest and sleep areas, look at them and ask yourself: Is there anything else I can do to make these areas feel peaceful, cozy, safe, and relaxing?

Toileting, Washing Up, Mealtime, and Food Preparation Areas

Mealtime and toileting areas must be clean, bright, and convenient for you and the children. That means the environment has to be easy to clean and sanitize and easy to work in, and the equipment should be scaled so that picking up, bending over, and reaching are kept to a minimum. Well-arranged food and toileting areas make your job as teacher easier. Food and toileting areas should be kept separate. However in many cases, a food preparation sink is attached to the same plumbing as a toileting or hand-washing sink. The pod design illustrated on page 27 is an example of effective use of plumbing and space to keep these areas separate. If you have to make environmental changes with a tight budget, directing your resources toward appropriate placement of diapering/toileting and food preparation areas is highly recommended. Effective plumbing makes a huge difference to the health and quality of experience of both children and teachers.

Toileting Area

An important activity, toileting is something children learn to do for themselves in due time. How you set up the space for diapering and toileting will make that learning easy or difficult.

Store all the diapers and supplies you need nearby. Also have next to the diaper-changing area a foot-operated or motion-sensitive wastebasket lined with a plastic liner for easy disposal. The diapering surface should be about 36 inches high. Making the surface easy to wash will help keep it germ-free. Supplies for cleaning and disinfecting should be readily available but out of reach of children.

If you use diaper table paper, have the roll at the end of the changing surface so you can easily throw away an old piece, clean and disinfect the surface, and then roll out a new one. The whole diapering setup needs to be close to a sink to promote hand-washing, and, of course, be separate from the food preparation area.

Diaper tables should have a 3-inch lip to prevent an infant from rolling off the table.

If toddlers are using bathrooms with toilets, child-sized toilets are preferable. Although using flush toilets is preferred, you can also set up a "potty area," also away from the food area, in a well-ventilated place near a toilet and warm running water. The area must be easily accessible in order to supervise toddlers. Provide more than one potty as two or three toddlers can sit on potties at the same time. The children can interact and learn from each other. Potties should not be cleaned in hand-washing sinks for children. Rather, they should be emptied into a toilet and cleaned in a utility sink. You will need toilet paper, paper towels, liquid soap, hand-washing facilities, and sanitizing supplies nearby.

When toddlers use a bathroom, they must have a teacher with them. The bathroom should be out of bounds or locked, when not in use, to keep toddlers from playing in there. Bathrooms with half-walls provide a sense of privacy while allowing teachers to visually supervise both inside and outside the bathroom area. This also provides a visual connection for other children when their primary care teacher is caring for another child.

The toileting area should be cheerful. Put pictures on the wall, and use some color to make the area bright. Make it a special place in which children know they are doing something valuable and important.

Washing Up Area

An ideal setting will have two or more low sinks with warm running water where toddlers can wash up. If you are installing new plumbing, consult a design professional about criteria for plumbing and specific measurements and requirements for sinks for infants and toddlers. In many cases, a sink is installed with the faucets to the side instead of at the back of the sink so children can reach them. A sink that is set into a cabinet may be harder to reach for a small child, so be sure to find out if the measurements will work before any construction takes place. If you have standard sinks, use sturdy stepping stools. Make sure the water temperature is 120 degrees Fahrenheit or lower. A single spigot, which blends warm and cold water, works well. If there are two faucets, you will need to plug and partially fill the sink for washing up. You must drain the sink, clean, and partially fill it again for each child who needs to wash up. You will have to watch the children; a toddler will turn the handles and may make the water too hot. The best way to control water temperature is to install temperature control devices on the hot-water heater or on the pipes leading to the sink. Some places have only cold water, which is safe but can be uncomfortable to use.

If you do not have a sink, use plastic tubs. Dishpan-sized tubs are good. You will have to empty, clean, sanitize, and refill the tub for each child. When filled with 3 inches of water, the tubs are steady. Set them on a low surface so toddlers can get their hands in easily; have soap nearby, and put a paper towel holder within the children's reach.

Washing up is an important activity, so avoid rushing the children. Set things up so children can feel the soap, see the bubbles, and watch their hands.

Eating Area

The eating area needs accessible storage and comfortable, easy-to-clean surfaces. The children need low, comfortable places to eat. In order to sit with the children while they eat, arrange a place for you to sit, too.

Low tables for up to four children work well and can be used for arts and crafts activities at other times. Consider tables that stack or fold out from the wall. You can use them for mealtimes, then store them away to enlarge the play space. Also consider using water tables or troughs with their covers on for food tables.

Young infants should be fed one at a time in the infant care teacher's arms, in a comfortable, adult-sized chair. A rocking chair is to be avoided, as it can hurt children playing on the floor. Have a table or shelf nearby to hold necessary items. As children become a little older, eating with one or two other infants can be enjoyable. Several options are available for feeding older infants. Ideally, meals and snacks are served at a child-sized table and small chairs or stools. A good guideline is to use the low table when an infant begins to climb onto and sit on the stool. You can leave a stool in the play area for infants to practice getting on and off.

For mobile and older infants, use child-sized tables and chairs. A table for infants from twelve to eighteen months of age should be about 12 to 14 inches high. Toddlers need a table 16 to 18 inches high

where they can sit and eat as well as stand and engage in messy play. When toddlers are seated, their feet should touch the floor. If their feet cannot touch the floor, the children will not feel stable while sitting and are likely to have trouble using their hands and arms easily. The table should be below chest height.

Toddlers will enjoy sitting in groups of two to four at small tables. Serve the food family style unless toddlers bring their own lunches. When children and adults eat together, they can have a social time. Natural wood tables sealed with a high-gloss coating are easy to clean. Sturdy chairs or backless stools are best. Backless stools work well for mobile infants and toddlers who can approach the stool from the back and straddle it in a comfortable wide-legged position. Other options include cube-type chairs with no legs, which take up a lot of space but when turned over can be used for other purposes. Stackable chairs or stools also allow for a more flexible environment.

Food Preparation Area

Before you set up the food preparation area, consider these five general guidelines:

1. Make sure that food and diapering areas are completely separate. That is one of the first requirements when you set up your environment. Change diapers at a location that has its own sink and is well ventilated. In a one-room center, make the food preparation area easy to reach, near a sink but separate from the diaper-changing area. This separation may be accomplished with a wall or half-wall. The floor in this area has to be nonskid and uncarpeted so it is easy to clean and sanitize. Provide adequate storage and shelving for bottle warmers, bibs, cups, and plates. Make the area cheerful by putting up pictures of

food and the names of the foods where the children can see them. If you have a separate kitchen, you may want to install a gate in the doorway. A gate that locks in place lets you get in to prepare the food but keeps wandering toddlers out. In a room with a pod design (see page 27), half walls and doors with Plexiglas can provide necessary separation while allowing children to see into the food preparation area.

2. Lock up all health hazards, such as bleach, cleaning supplies, and first aid supplies, that are in low cupboards. A better option is to store hazardous items in cupboards over 4 feet high.

3. Make sure the floors are not slippery. Use low-gloss wax, fill in any cracks between tiles, or put in some kind of nonskid flooring. Do not have carpets in the food preparation area. Floors should be easy to clean and dry quickly.

4. Have adults-only work areas and storage spaces that are too high for children to reach.

5. Make sure all surfaces and equipment are easy to clean and sanitize. Knowing that cleaning up is easy encourages you to let toddlers learn to eat by themselves, even if they do make a mess. Easy-to-clean surfaces and equipment also reduce the time you need to spend cleaning. If the eating area doubles for messy play, you might have "messy trays" stacked on a shelf nearby. These plastic trays have a lip to keep things such as shaving cream and finger paints in the tray.

Storage and Shelves

Storage is the teacher's strong silent partner in a smoothly run child care program. The ease and efficiency that result from having well-organized storage make building storage into your environmental planning well worthwhile.

Wise Use of Storage

Keep items and materials near the area in which they are needed, for example, diapering materials near the changing area or the potties, playthings in the play area.

Make stored items easy to access. If things are hard to reach, they require extra effort to bring out. The same goes for the children's playthings.

Label all storage shelves and bins with both the words and pictures of the items. You can protect the pictures by covering them with clear adhesive paper.

Transparent containers allow toddlers to see what is inside. Remember: you do not need lots of blocks for a toddler; a few blocks should be enough for the child to work with and not be overwhelmed. A basket with five or six stacking blocks, connecting pieces, or sorting objects is better for the child and for you. Another option is to use tray containers with handles, so then toddlers can both see into

the trays and carry them easily. For small items, use containers that are easy for toddlers to handle so they can carry the items from the shelf to a play surface without your help and without spilling the toys.

Teachers' Storage

Teachers' storage should be designed so it will not interfere with infants' and toddlers' movements or explorations. Build open or closed shelves on any wall over 4 feet high. The overhead shelving can be installed anywhere in the room and make good use of empty wall space.

High shelves can be used for additional toys and equipment. You will want to store some toys so you can bring out the "new" and store the "old" playthings every so often. Being out of sight for a while is what makes toys "new." Use closed storage to rotate toys and to hold equipment you do not use all the time: recorded music, extra art materials, and paper. Equipment you need often for changing, cooking, and playing can go on high open shelves where you can easily see and reach the items.

A large locked closet or cabinet is helpful for storing bulk supplies. Teachers also need to store personal belongings out of the children's reach. Ideally, an area should be set aside for teachers only.

Changing and Food Storage Areas

The changing area must have handy storage, with such supplies as diapers and ointments for diaper rash placed out of reach of infants and toddlers. Use a step trash can for the diaper area, but make sure that toddlers cannot get to it throughout the day. You must be able to reach all needed supplies easily without leaving the child you are changing.

If the families supply the diapers, you need to store each child's diaper supplies nearby so you can reach them from the changing table or pick them up on the way. In either case, convenience is vital; diaper bags cannot be piled four deep or be put one behind the other so that you cannot see all of them. Make sure the child's name is written in big letters on the bag or on a large plastic tag. You can store diapers and other supplies for each child in a labeled basket above the changing table.

The food area needs convenient storage, too. Items must be easy for you to get quickly, but they must be out of infants' and toddlers' reach. Open-shelf storage (over 4 feet high) with a small lip meets those needs. The children can see the items but cannot reach them. You can see what you need and reach it easily. Make sure the shelves are not too deep as things may be hidden from view. With all shelving and storage, follow recommendations for earthquake safety.

Medication is frequently stored in the food preparation area, particularly if it needs to be refrigerated. According to the California Childcare Health Program's Health & Safety Note on "Medication Administration in Child Care Programs," medications should be stored in their original container in a secure place out of the reach of children. Prescription medication should be stored in a plastic zip-lock bag in the food section of the refrigerator. Also, medications that are controlled substances should be locked up, and the key should be monitored closely.

Child-sized Storage

Being able to see playthings is what invites children to play. Anita Olds, an expert on infant environments, says, "Well-organized storage and display of materials, which enable children to see what is available, where it belongs, and where to use it, are critical to the success of most activities."

The size and shape of shelves really matter. Those that are too long and hold too many items can confuse a toddler. Those with compartments, shutters, and drawers frustrate younger infants.

Simple, custom-built units can be cheaper than shelving available for purchase. Decide what you need; then design it. If one of the family members has carpentry skills, perhaps you can get him or her to make the shelves you need to fit your space.

Shelves that are not well designed may allow a child to try climbing them. To discourage climbing, make the second shelf high enough so that it is hard to pull up on. This shelf should be as high as the midpoint between the toddler's elbow and shoulder. Put the next shelf 10 to 12 inches higher. Use vertical dividers on the bottom shelf. If they are wide apart, a toddler can climb in and curl up, making the shelving something to explore. Dividers on the upper shelves can go close together to discourage climbing between them.

Put small shelves in playpits and on decks and platforms. Toys that children use there can be stored on those shelves.

Use natural wood for shelving. The wood shows off the toys and lets infants and toddlers see and feel a natural material. Pine is inexpensive and works well. A small shelf will hold 12 or so toys. For infants, make the shelf 28 inches wide by 20 inches high by 10 inches deep, with two levels. Shelves for toddlers can be as high as 30 inches and have three levels— a bottom, middle, and top shelf. The top shelf can be used for toys, too. Lower shelves can also be used with one layer of shelving below and the top surface open like a table. Children can cruise along these and use the top surface as a work space for puzzles and other small-motor manipulatives.

Wooden cubbies or plastic bins, good for infants' and toddlers' belongings, must be low and small. For children's outside wear, use hooks placed low enough for toddlers to reach on their own.

Maintaining Order

Creative use of storage is vital for maintaining order. Be creative about storage ideas. Use netting hung on the wall above 4 feet to store balls, foam pieces, and extra pillows. Zippered pillowcases or pillow covers labeled with a laundry marker can be used to store dress-up clothes, pieces of fabric, painting aprons, and other soft items.

Use wheeled carts, toy boxes, or milk crates to gather up toys. Then put the toys back on the shelves where they belong. Toys that do not have storage space may get lost or broken.

Involve the children. Give toddlers empty buckets or other small containers labeled with pictures of plastic interlocking blocks, toy cars, or other small items. Encourage the children to collect the things that go in their bucket.

Outdoor Space

Direct access to the outdoors can allow use of the outdoor space all day long. Your design and use of the outdoor space will be greatly affected by the climate. For instance, in areas where it gets very cold in the winter, a space between the outdoors and the indoors may be used as a mudroom for boots, jackets, and equipment. In more temperate climates, you may have the equivalent of an outdoor classroom where children can spend many hours of the day outdoors. In some places, protection from the sun is a priority, and in others blocking wind or maximizing sun exposure for warmth is important. Whatever your climate, creating environmental variety is as important outside as it is inside. Variety in the outdoor area can be in textures, surfaces, movement, equipment, and slopes.

Here are some of the things you will want to have in the outside play area:

blankets	dirt
ramps	trees
boulders	drinking water
sand	tunnels
bushes	grass
shade	water for play
climbers	hills
slides	wheel toys

Ideally, a playroom will open directly to an outside play area. If you have no outside play area, you will have to improvise. Use local parks, have stroller parades, and take nature walks in the neighborhood.

If you do have an outdoor area, think of it as an infant/toddler park. The area will be different from an outdoor area for pre-schoolers. Because children from young infancy to three years of age will all play there, the area needs to meet many different developmental needs. A three-month-old needs to be in a protected area that allows the child to move freely and look around. A ten-month-old will need space to crawl and things to pull up onto. A toddler will be moving over large parts of the yard quickly. A child with disabilities or other special needs may benefit from some adaptations such as an extra handrail for balancing or a wagon to get around. Ask yourself: How can this space meet the needs, interests, and developing abilities of all the children?

Grass or Soft Ground Cover

You need a shaded place to spread blankets for young infants and to let crawling infants roam—a soft, grassy area is ideal. A lawn encourages toddlers to roll, tumble, and relax. The grass needs to be inspected regularly because young children will put anything they find in their mouths. You can use different kinds of grasses for variety or cut the grass to different lengths. In some places, you can plant mosses or special grasses to provide a thick, springy surface. Check with your local county agricultural agent or a local nursery to find out what natural ground covers grow well in your area. Remember that the ground cover will get a lot of wear, so it has to be tough. Some programs have installed artificial grass as a ground cover. It gives the softer feel of grass, wears well, and requires limited maintenance. Plan for a good drainage system, so that water does not collect on the playing surface.

Use large, round boulders for variety, or plant shrubs to make a miniature forest. Infants and toddlers can wander in the "trees." Logs and benches on the grass give young children something to climb on and teachers a place to sit or lean against while they watch or play with the children.

Protection from Hazards

Outdoor play has to be safe, for the outdoors can be dangerous. To keep infants and toddlers away from passing cars and bicycles, you will need to fence the outside area with a gate that children cannot open. But think also about the dangers inside the yard too, and remove any hazards. For example, all the plants in the area must be safe. People who sell plants usually know only the major poisonous ones. They do not know what will happen if an infant chews the leaf of an ordinary shrub. You need to know. To find out, contact your local poison control center. Look in the phone book or call your local hospital for the number. Each season can present safety hazards: from icy sidewalks to burning hot slides. Check for hazards throughout the year as different plants bloom and surfaces change. Before planting a tree in the yard, consider whether it might be a known source of allergens for children in your care.

Other hazards include gravel, small rocks, wild mushrooms growing on old wood, and uncovered sand areas. Areas should be kept free of animal waste, insects, rodents, and other pests. Cats treat any sand or loose dirt as a giant litter box. If you have a sandbox or sand area, cover it when you are not outside. You can use a tarpaulin or a wooden frame covered with mesh wire. Store the cover outside the play area during playtimes. Pest control can be achieved by using non-toxic products or by using Integrated Pest Management techniques (see page 75 in the Suggested Resources section for more information).

Barriers and Pathways

Pathways and barriers direct traffic outside just as they do inside. Before installing pathways, think about the yard. Make a list of every activity you want to have; then decide how much space you can allow for each. Surround the infant area with developmental barriers, such as those described in the Glossary. Place developmental barriers between the sand and grass so infants too young for sand will stay on the grass.

You can use low rocks or wooden walls as barriers. You might also use poles, kiln-dried wood, or peeler logs. Check to see that they have not been treated with hazardous substances and are free of splinters. Other options include a slatted walkway of wood: a wooden platform about 18 inches wide and 3 inches high, with some space between the slats. Young crawlers usually will not go over the walkway, but toddlers will. A barrier of shrubs also stops crawlers, whereas toddlers will push through it.

Surfaces for Rolling Toys

Toddlers need a smooth surface (concrete or blacktop) for wheeled toys. Trucks, tricycles, low-riding vehicles, and wagons for pulling all have to move easily over the ground. Try to include doll strollers, miniature shopping carts, and pull toys in your collection.

Consider designing a pathway that has grass on both sides to provide a smooth place to ride. In this way, you will not cover too much of the area with a hard surface. A circular traffic pathway wide enough for two bikes and that curves around the play yard is ideal. The teacher needs to be able to see the entire pathway from any place in the yard. The path has to work for strollers, too, so infants in strollers can enjoy a smooth ride around the yard.

Texture Walks or Paths

A texture walk is a regular pathway or a special area with various surfaces whose purpose is to give toddlers variety and practice with different materials. For texture walks, you can use almost anything: dirt, wood rounds, patterned rock, bricks, sanded planks, half-logs, cobblestones, sand, bark, stepping stones, or rubberized studded tiles. Make the path about 2 feet

wide and each section about 4 feet long. You can also change the railings by using chains, rope, pickets, poles, or plastic piping.

For crawlers, avoid using anything that is too rough. Use sanded wood or wood rounds. Try grass of different colors or other ground covers, making sure they are not poisonous.

Use of Nature for Learning

You have a wonderful ally in Mother Nature, an old and wise teacher. Everyone learns from nature. Therefore, include as much variety of natural objects as you can.

If you are starting from scratch on a play yard, plant some trees that lose their leaves annually so the children can see them fall and get blown about by the wind. For variety, plant trees or shrubs that stay green all year. Remember to plant some that blossom in the spring. When you plant, think about the seasons: What plants

change with the seasons? Consider planting something that smells wonderful and would be safe if a child decides to chew on it.

Consider creating sunny and shaded areas. Shade both protects children and teaches them about temperature. An area shaded by shrubs feels different from being in a sunny place.

Wind socks and wind chimes hung outside help children learn about the wind. Banners or colored cloth streamers move in a breeze, too.

Large flat boulders let infants and toddlers explore stone. They can climb over the rocks, look at their shapes, and lean against them. If you can put in a trough to hold water, do so, using wood, metal, or stone. Drip water from a hose into the trough.

Hills teach children about balance and going up and down. Hills hide some things, show other things. If you have a hill, you are lucky. If not, consider building and seeding a small hill with grass. As the children watch grass grow, they learn more about nature.

Covered Area for Rain and Sun

Infants and toddlers need to play outside year-round. When it rains, the children need a sheltered place to play. In the summer sun, they need a cool place to play. Before you plan for shade, think about the direction of the sun in relation to the play yard. What areas are sunny when you are outdoors? Do you already have a shady area?

Some centers have awnings on the main building. Many homes have covered porches or decks. Areas containing any metal play equipment need to be protected from too much sun. Slides in open, sunny areas should face north to reduce direct sun contact, keeping the surfaces from becoming too hot. You can use waterproof tarps or cloth to create shade. Another possibility is to build a lath house by securing thin, flat pieces of wood together on a wooden frame, to easily create a shady spot. You can also create a large cube with long PVC pipes and clip sheets or canvas to make a portable shade structure.

A playhouse with a roof is another option. You can build one in the middle of the yard. The playhouse can double as a storage shed for riding toys, planks, parachutes, wagons, balls, and sand or water toys. If the yard is right next to the child care center, put up a lean-to using the main outside wall. Add two walls and a sloping roof, and you have a covered area.

Messy Activities

A wooden deck or flooring, ideal for outside messy play, also drains water fast. Thus a deck will be dry enough for play sooner than wet grass. If the deck is high, it gives young children a chance to see things from a higher place.

Because messes are easier to clean up outside, plan to do some messy play activities outdoors. Simply wash away traces of paint or clay with a hose. On sunny days, painting or working with clay or play dough is better done in the shade; the sun dries things out too fast. The sun is ideal for water play, however. Buckets and basins of water and some plastic cups and spoons are all that is needed for children to play with.

Toddlers like to use large pieces of chalk to mark smooth cement. You can help children make roads for their riding toys. Children can also paint their cars with colored water and wash them with soapy water and sponges.

Books, Music, and Dramatic Play

The outdoors can be a perfect theater. The children can sit on the grass to sing or play music, sprawl on a hillside to watch

someone perform, or curl up with you in the shade to hear a story or look at a book. Nature books are excellent for reading outside.

Playing dress-up games outdoors is a special treat. The firefighter can have a real hose. The shopper can push a shopping cart. The car driver can race around orange safety cones. The police officer can stop traffic with a sign and a whistle.

You may have to bring out equipment for these activities. Because most equipment cannot be left outside, you may want to use a large cart on wheels to carry the equipment or install outdoor storage cabinets. Make the sides of the cart low enough so toddlers can put things back in the cart at clean-up time.

Low-cost Outdoor Equipment

Low-cost equipment includes benches, plastic milk crates, inflatables, such as inner tubes, mattresses, big balls, small balls, and tires, and wide sanded boards. The boards should be short enough for toddlers to lift and carry or drag. Children can also build with the boards and the plastic milk crates. Toddlers like to stack, put things in, push and pull, and sit in the milk crates. Buckets of water and paint-brushes can be used to paint fences and stones.

You can bury tires sideways so a half-circle protrudes and works as a small tunnel or a place to sit on or lean against. Make a row of half-circles to form a pathway railing for cruisers. If your area is sunny, paint the tires a light color to cut down on the heat they absorb. Painting the inside of tires a light color will discourage spiders from spinning webs there. Drilling several holes in the part of the tires you plan to bury will help water to drain.

If you have a hill, you can build an inexpensive slide right in it. This is the safest possible kind of slide because there is nowhere to fall.

Section Four:

Accommodations for Children with Disabilities or Other Special Needs

The following recommendations support caring for infants and toddlers with disabilities in inclusive settings.

Physical Disabilities (Orthopedic Impairments)

There are many different ways to support a child with physical disabilities in an inclusive setting.

Pace

For some children, there is a delay between the intention to do something and actually doing it. Encourage the child to become as involved as much as possible in caregiving routines and exploration but do not hurry the child. Hurrying a child with cerebral palsy, for example, may trigger tightening of muscles and make an activity, such as diapering or eating, difficult. Sudden movements may also be counterproductive.

Positioning

Special chairs or positioning equipment may be needed throughout the day, requiring extra space. Positioning is how the child's body is placed when in a stationary position. This technique can help children be more successful when engaged in activities and often helps them achieve more normal muscle tone.

Position children who need it so they feel comfortable and secure during routines and play. Find out from parents the best positioning strategies. Think about how a child can be supported but able to exert efforts on his own. Be sensitive to when the position needs to change. Not being able to get out of a position can be frustrating. Sometimes what seems like a psychological insecurity may, in fact, be a physical insecurity that can be remedied by correct positioning or support.

Providing for Movement

Familiarize the child with the environment and how best to move within it. Space may be needed to accommodate movement of special equipment such as a walker or a wheelchair. Safety considerations include providing a clear path—smooth but not slippery surfaces—and ways around thick rugs inside or sand

Note: Excerpted/Adapted from Donna Sullivan and Janet Gonzales-Mena, "Beginning Together Training Manual" (unpublished, 2003).

areas outside. Keep the environment free of clutter.

Though most children who are typically developing go from crawling to cruising to walking, some children in an inclusive program may need ways to cruise later or longer than typically developing children. Arrange the room so there are supports for cruising such as furniture, tables, rails, or walls to pull up on and use for support. Make sure these are sturdy and at the appropriate height.

Providing for Play and Exploration

Place toys within reach but not necessarily in the infant's or toddler's hand. Encourage the child to reach out. Move toys to low, accessible shelves. Provide toys that children with delays in fine motor development can grasp, move, or create an effect by using. Modify toys and materials when necessary (see below).

Support, encourage, and facilitate interactions with toys. Rather than using direct instruction to show how something works, tickle the child's curiosity and wait to see if he or she becomes engaged. Some children with physical disabilities have not had some of the play opportunities that their typically developing peers have had.

Support, encourage, and facilitate interactions with peers. Accept different levels of interaction as appropriate to each individual. Watch for subtle responses. Sometimes just being near other children is interactive enough.

Adapting Materials, Toys, and Utensils

The following suggestions are ways to adapt playthings and utensils for a child with a disability.

- Nonskid materials keep toys, utensils, and such from slipping. Use re-attachable fabric fasteners, nonskid pads, and suction soap holders.

- Make handles bigger with foam bike handle grips, cotton pads, "vet wrap," or duct tape.
- Add handles, for example, cork stoppers or wooden knobs on puzzle pieces and glue tongue depressors on cardboard book pages for easy turning.
- Bend spoon handles, use flexible straws, and use nontipping or spouted cups with lids to make eating more independent.
- Enlarge the holes in beads or use stiffer string (cover the end with masking tape).
- Cover paper materials (books, cards) with clear contact paper to protect them from the drool of infants and toddlers.
- Use magnetic blocks.

Visual Impairments

The following recommendations will help you to support a child with visual impairments to have full participation in the program.

Providing for Movement

Familiarize the child with the environment. Keep the room arrangement consistent so infants and toddlers with visual limitations can move more easily. Minimize clutter.

To help crawlers and toddlers navigate the room, look for ways in which they can be as independent as possible by using auditory and tactile cues as guides.

Providing for Play and Exploration

Play with real objects is especially important for the child with a visual impairment. Concrete learning is critical, and the transition between what is real and what is a toy is very difficult without visual input.

Place objects within reach, and help the child know they are there by touch or other types of cues. Encourage the child to reach out. Toys should be placed on low, accessible shelves. Support, encourage, and facilitate interactions with objects. Engage the child's curiosity by selecting items with high contrast or that provide auditory input. Expand play behaviors if play is limited to mouthing or smelling.

Add textured cues (sandpaper, fake fur, vinyl) to help children locate items. Toys that children can grasp, move, or use to create an effect are good. Modify toys and materials when necessary to add auditory elements (a bell in a foam ball) or additional texture. Adding smells may make toys and objects more identifiable and interesting.

Make the most of residual visual abilities by using toys that light up (use caution if the child is prone to seizures) or have highly contrasting colors or heavy black outlines. Place objects on something with a high-contrast background or defined edge (tray).

Support, encourage, and facilitate interactions with peers. The child with a visual impairment may not be aware of another child nearby. Adults can provide support by speaking and through touch. Direction words (left, right) are used early on to determine location.

Hearing Impairments

Children with hearing impairments can participate fully in your program with a few adaptations.

Multisensory Experiences

- Use multisensory cues.
- Use visual and tactile cues to help guide the infant or toddler in daily routines and activities.
- Use picture cues with older toddlers to show how materials are used or to help toddlers tell you what they want.
- Position the infant or toddler so that there is a clear view of the speaker. Lighting is important as it illuminates the face of the speaker.

Residual Auditory Abilities

If a child can hear a particular sound, such as a bell, use it when appropriate to get the child's attention. It is important to learn individual ways of using whatever hearing the child has in order to foster independence and interaction with others. It is also important that the child becomes aware of those sounds that are within his capacity.

If the child has a hearing aid, the teacher must learn how to check it daily and change the battery as needed. The teacher must also know how to put the aid in the child's ear. Many young children do not want to wear their hearing aids, and a plan should be developed with the family members to help the child get used to wearing them consistently.

Play and Exploration

Support and facilitate interactions with toys and with peers. Use simple sign language with all children so that they are able to communicate with one another in a nonverbal way.

Provide toys that are visually interesting that children can grasp, move, or use to create an effect. Modify toys and materials, when necessary, to make them more interesting or to create curiosity in the child.

Emotional or Behavioral Challenges

The following recommendations can help you to make adaptations for a child with emotional or behavioral challenges.

Clarity, Consistency, and Predictability

Teach children clear and consistent limits. Model the behaviors you want to establish. Give children the words to express their feelings and acknowledge their right to have those feelings. Explanations should be brief and direct.

Provide space for privacy for children to move in and out of their own accord as needed while still being supervised by an adult. Some children need time alone to regain their composure.

Some toddlers are helped by having concrete cues for transitions to alert them to what is going to happen next, such as ringing a bell to indicate when the play yard is available or showing pictures of the next activity (snack).

Encouraging Play and Exploration

Be aware of individual thresholds of stimulation. Some infants and toddlers do better with reduced stimulation and limited choices.

Most toddlers feel more secure when an adult is nearby, especially if they know they can depend on that adult to provide focus and control when needed. It is especially important to provide that control before a child damages materials or hurts another child.

Support, encourage, and facilitate interactions with toys and peers. Accept different levels of interaction as appropriate to each individual, and establish limits for a child who needs them.

Developmental Disabilities

During caregiving routines and exploration periods, encourage the child to become involved. Explain what will happen, and wait for the child to indicate in some way that the message ("I'm going to change your diaper") was received. Give plenty of time for the child to do whatever he or she can do to help. Allow the child to keep trying even when frustration arises, but be sensitive to how much frustration he or she can tolerate.

Providing for Movement

Familiarize the child with the environment. Provide tactile, auditory, and visual cues as guides. For the child who is not yet walking independently, provide opportunities to move in whatever way he or she can.

Create Multisensory Experiences

Although multisensory experiences are important for all infants and toddlers, those with developmental disabilities may need additional experiences and space that invites open-ended exploration and play.

Use language to help guide the infant or toddler in daily routines and activities. Picture cues show how materials are used or help toddlers tell you what they want if they do not have language or gestures to do it.

Capitalize on Strengths

Support the child's successes and give approval without distracting the child from his success or activity. Play/activity sequences may need to be broken down into smaller steps.

Provide for open-ended play and exploration. Be aware of safety considerations for a child who may be developing at a different rate (one who may still put things in his mouth).

All infants and toddlers need plenty of open-ended play and exploration, but some may not know what to do when provided with the opportunity in a safe and interesting environment. Help them by gently giving encouragement, by making sure toys and materials are enticing and adapted to their abilities, and by giving them some ideas about what to do with the toys and materials. Model, if necessary. Think about ways to stimulate children's curiosity and motivate them to explore.

Support, encourage, and facilitate the child's interactions with toys and other children. Accept different levels of interaction as appropriate to each individual.

Model appropriate interactions and behaviors. Describe interactions in simple terms.

Allow for Extra Time and Repeated Practice

Children learn best through practice and repetition. Children with developmental delays often need more opportunities to practice when learning new skills. For a skill to be mastered, it must be practiced many times and over several days or weeks. Provide encouragement to keep children engaged while they work toward mastery.

Section Five:
Practical Tips

Setting up a child care environment involves practical considerations. This section offers tips on design of the facility and selection of furnishings.

Air, Light, and Heating

Air, light, and heat are the background workhorses vital to the environment yet easily overlooked. Good heat is essential to the health and comfort of a child care setting. A wonderful modern feature is a heated floor, which can make a big difference for infants and also for you since you are often on the floor with the children. With every type of heating, the temperature should be adjustable and adequate (65 to 75 degrees Fahrenheit in winter and 68 to 82 degrees Fahrenheit in summer). A moderately low setting is best. When the room is too warm, both you and the children may feel sluggish. The furnace also needs to be maintained and checked regularly.

Fresh air is essential and has to circulate evenly so that crawling infants get some but are not chilled. One way to ensure everyone gets enough healthful fresh air is to go outside several times a day. Another way is to open windows or screened sliding glass doors. If the air is too dry, you may need a humidifier.

Lighting is crucial to health. All people need some natural light to regulate their bodily functions. Light is also a major source of stimulation for the senses. Research on people who spend hours indoors each day, in front of televisions or under fluorescent lights, shows that too little natural light is unhealthy.

All indoor settings, however, need some artificial lighting, and numerous options are available. The healthiest course is to copy nature. Full-spectrum lighting is close to natural sunlight. Use full-spectrum bulbs or a mixture of fluorescent and incandescent lights to achieve full-spectrum lighting. If local fire codes permit, hanging fabric from the ceiling or walls can soften light, particularly for young infants, who spend a lot of time gazing up. Pink fabric can help balance out the intensity of fluorescent lights. Compact fluorescent bulbs have a longer life, use less energy, and fit into the same sockets as incandescent light bulbs. Connect lights to adjustable dimmers so you can easily change the brightness. Mix lighting styles, too. Use lamps, overhead built-in lights, windows, skylights, open doors with screens, and French doors. Different styles create different effects. For example, small local lights give a warm, cozy feeling. Built-in overheads are cooler, but light an entire room.

Boxes and Barrels

A cardboard appliance container or barrel can be lined with fabric or low-pile carpet. Cut out windows and a door before lining the container. Then put an activity box, a few toys, or a texture quilt inside. This can be a private space for one child or a playing space for two.

A few large cartons can make a temporary boundary. This "instant wall" will create two smaller playing spaces. Cut out doors so children can enter in one side and come out the other, or use two or three cartons to create a place for dramatic play. Smaller boxes can be painted to look like stoves and refrigerators. Larger boxes form the walls; the insides of the boxes can become other rooms or closets for a playhouse.

Turn a barrel or box on its side, open both ends, and line it with a variety of fabrics. Using nontoxic glue, paste down any loose edges. You have now created a crawling tunnel with many textures!

A cardboard tube from a roll of carpet can be used as a tunnel for toy cars or balls. A plastic rain gutter also works and offers a different experience because children can see and stop the cars as they roll down.

Home improvement stores are good sources of materials. They may give away old wallpaper sample books, which are full of different patterns, textures, and colors. The stores also have sample books of fabrics.

Carpets

A low-pile carpet is easier to clean, and small toys and dirt are easily visible. Get a hypoallergenic carpet, if possible. To avoid any inhalation of fumes, exercise all recommended precautions associated with carpet installation. This often means airing out a newly carpeted room for a period of time before using it. When you choose colors, avoid really dark or very light shades as they both show dirt more than a neutral tone. Odd colors or those that are too bright are to be avoided. Infants, toddlers, and teachers have to live with these colors for many hours each day.

Rug manufacturers or outlets and large fabric stores often are good sources of free or low-cost remnants. Those places usually have small pieces of carpet that will cover one area. Carpeted platforms of different heights can challenge crawling infants. Use different textures to create different moods. Make a carpeted ramp, or build up carpeted levels around a waterbed or playpit.

Ceilings

Use the ceiling to hang banners, mobiles, posters, and wind chimes. If the ceiling is strong enough, you can hang grids made from wooden slats. Adjust the grids to different heights, and hang playthings from them. A simple alternative is to put a single beam across the narrowest point in the room. In a square room, this will be a corner. Hang things for the children that they can play with or look at and that meet local fire codes.

Changeable Environment

A changeable environment is one that is easy to rearrange. Children from birth to three years of age change so much themselves that their environment has to keep up with them.

The empty space in the center of the room constitutes a changeable environment that is like a stage set to be altered as needed. Use simple, low-cost, lightweight equipment to change the setting: cardboard boxes, plastic laundry baskets, air mattresses, pillows, mats, toys, large balls, plastic milk crates, and piles of pillows.

You can also change the environment by rotating toys in and out of storage. Store and rotate toys on a regular schedule, maybe weekly or once a month.

Cleanliness

Cleanliness is essential in a child care setting. A clean environment supports safety, health, convenience, and harmony. The secret to cleanliness in a child care setting is to make cleaning easy yet thorough and to clean throughout the day. An easy-to-clean environment means you can spend your best energy with the children, not in cleaning up after them. Ask yourself if you feel confident to put your mouth on toys or surfaces as the infants do. If not, create a new cleaning system that would instill that confidence.

Look at everything you are thinking of placing in the setting. Can each item be cleaned thoroughly and easily in a dishwasher, washing machine, or by hand? Would something else that could work as well be easier to clean?

To make cleaning easy, use washable covers on furniture and pillows and have easy-to-wipe surfaces. Buy equipment that is simply designed. A food blender with one on-off button is easier to keep clean than one that looks like a jet control panel. A climber play structure with simple, smooth pieces is better than one with lots of small breakable parts.

Mealtime and diapering areas need special attention. They get the dirtiest and have to be kept sanitized.

Cushions

Use closed-cell foam for pillows. It does not absorb moisture, which breeds germs, and the foam is easy to clean. Make or buy removable covers with zippers or re-attachable fabric fasteners for fast, easy washing. Mix the colors, sizes, and shapes as much as possible. You can also make a set of blocks using pieces of foam covered with various kinds of materials.

Floor Surfaces

Provide a smooth surface for toddlers' riding toys. Use low-pile carpets in areas where children engage in small-muscle activities. Make sure that rug edges are firmly attached to the floor. Create texture walks using mats of thick plastic with various textures (ribs, small ridges, and bumps). Use linoleum, or other easy-to-clean floor coverings, in eating, food preparation, diaper-changing, and messy activity areas.

Custodial Support

Draw up a clear, well-labeled floor plan for the custodians or others who help clean. Explain why things are arranged the way they are so the staff members will not leave furniture in one corner after they have cleaned the room. You can also help them to understand that children will be mouthing things in the room, so nontoxic cleaning supplies and good rinsing make a crucial difference.

Light and Texture Variations

Introduce variety in sources of light. Build platforms at windows so children are near natural light. Use full-spectrum bulbs, which are like sunshine. Employ general, task-specific, floor, wall, ceiling, and desk lighting.

Wall-mounted light fixtures reflect light, washing it toward the ceiling and down the wall for a soft look. Wall lights convey a feeling of being surrounded by light, as though one were outside in nature.

Use mirrors to add variety and light. Plexiglas mirrors are the safest and can be ordered cut to any size. Mirrors should be large enough (about 30 inches to 40 inches high and 40 inches wide) so two children can see themselves from head to toe. This sight of themselves supports children's developing sense of self.

Vary the textures on floors, walls, and furniture. When you choose floor coverings, select a variety: smooth vinyl, smooth low-pile rugs, textured low-pile rugs, and so on. Place heavy plastic mats with different textures over the carpets. You can add textures by changing what is on the walls. Create texture quilts for infants, using velvet, satin, and cotton fabric in a variety of colors. Put cellophane under some of the quilt sections so they make a noise when pressed. Different fabrics and colors for small throw pillows add variety.

Limited Space

Designing a small area that needs to meet the varied needs of infants and toddlers is a challenge. The following strategies may be used:

- A flexible environment
- Lightweight, easy-to-change boundaries
- Multiuse, multipurpose equipment
- Multilevel structures
- Optimal storage and the creative use of space

Tables that serve two or three purposes, such as eating, art play, and messy activities, are examples of multipurpose equipment. Another example is covered foam shapes that serve as boundaries and as seats for teachers.

Using neglected space is a great strategy for a small area. For example, the space from the ceiling down about 6 feet often goes unused. Install storage cabinets, windows, or skylights. A banner, mobile, canopy, or kite can brighten a dark corner.

Designing a child care setting with limited space is like taking a long trip in a small boat. You have to plan everything ahead of time to use the small space in the best possible way.

Overstimulation

To soften noise, use plenty of soft furnishings and coverings that absorb sound. Some construction companies or office furnishing companies may have extra scraps of material to help absorb reverberating sound in a space. This practice is especially helpful to soften noise from other groups of children nearby. Remember to place sound-absorbing materials near the source of the sound rather than in the area you want to have quiet. Avoid too much light, especially harsh artificial light, but allow as much natural light as possible.

The following considerations may help you decide to cut down on stimulation:

- Are there separate places for quiet and noisy activities?
- Are those areas far enough apart?
- Is it hard to think clearly because of the noise?
- Are parts of the room cluttered or disorderly?

Home Away from Home

Every infant/toddler program is going to have a unique feel to it. Personal, cultural, and socioeconomic differences contribute to the uniqueness of each program. This book offers guidance for making the best use of resources, space, and knowledge of child development to create a home away from home for each infant and toddler in your care.

Suggested Resources

Articles and Books

American Academy of Pediatrics. *Caring for Our Children: National Health and Safety Performance Standards Guidelines for Out-of-Home Child Care.* 2nd ed. Elk Grove Village, IL: American Academy of Pediatrics, 2002.

Caring for Our Children is the most comprehensive source of information available on the development and evaluation of the health and safety aspects of day care and child care centers. The guidelines address the health and safety needs of children ranging in age from infants to twelve-year-olds. There are eight chapters of 658 standards and a ninth chapter of 48 recommendations for licensing and community agencies and organizations. The book and other health and safety resources may also be accessed at the National Center for Health and Safety in Child Care and Early Education at http://nrc.uchsc.edu/. A six-part video series (1995) is also available.

Balk, Sophie, and Ruth Etzel. *Handbook of Pediatric Environmental Health.* 2nd ed. Elk Grove Village, IL: American Academy of Pediatrics, 2003.

A tool for identifying, treating, and preventing pediatric environmental health hazards, this second edition updates and expands the scope of the text with 10 new chapters covering emerging environmental threats, updated content for a wide range of health hazards, and much more.

Bergen, Doris, Rebecca Reid, and Louis Torelli. *Educating and Caring for Very Young Children: The Infant/Toddler Curriculum.* New York: Teachers College Press, 2000.

The early childhood education series includes floor plans for three "educare" spaces and expands on the idea of curriculum as a dynamic, responsive experience rather than a rigid learning structure.

Bunnett, Rochelle, and others. "Environments for Special Needs: Beginning Workshop." *Child Care Information Exchange* 114 (March/April 1997): 41–50, 55–64.

Five articles examine the creation of environments that address children's special needs: (1) "Getting to the Heart of the Matter" (on changing from a deficit model to a competence model); (2) "Enhancing the Environment for All Children"; (3) "Using Your Senses to Adapt Environments"; (4) "More Than a Playground: Accessible Outdoor Learning Centers"; and (5) "Interest Areas Support Individual Learning."

Child Development Resources (1993). *SpecialCare Curriculum and Trainer's Manual*, PO Box 280, Norge, VA 23127-0280; (757) 566-3300

Cook, R. E., A. Tessier, and M. D. Klein. *Adapting Early Childhood Curricula for Children in Inclusive Settings.* 5th ed. Upper Saddle River, NJ: Prentice Hall, 2000.

Dombro, Amy Laura, Laura J. Colker, and Diane Trister Dodge. *The Creative Curriculum for Infants and Toddlers.* Washington, DC: Teaching Strategies, Inc., 1999.

Chapter 7 addresses such topics as creating a welcoming environment, reflecting home culture, planning a responsive environment, defining play areas outdoors, and adapting the environment for children with special needs. This book is available in Spanish.

Godwin, Annabelle, and Lorraine Schrag. *Setting Up for Infant/Toddler Care: Guidelines for Centers and Family Child Care Homes.* Rev. ed. Washington, DC: National Association for the Education of Young Children, 1996.

Experts describe how to work with parents, keep children safe and healthy, and promote all areas of their development. This book includes job descriptions, staffing schedules, budgets, and discussion of family child care systems and satellite child care homes. Two chapters focus on the environment: "Setting up the Environment" and "Infant and Toddler Care in Family Child Care Homes."

Gonzalez-Mena, Janet, and Dianne Eyer. *Infants, Toddlers, and Caregivers: A Curriculum of Respectful, Responsive Care and Education.* New York: McGraw-Hill, 2003.

This text is a practical introduction to the principles and practices of caregiving for infants and toddlers. It combines a child-centered philosophy with problem-solving strategies and provides a thorough discussion of gender role stereotyping and multicultural issues in child care. The philosophy of caregiving that underlies this book comes from Magda Gerber and Tom Forrest, M.D., as well as the earlier work of Emmi Pikler. These pioneers of the field stressed the need to integrate (1) knowledge of play as curriculum, (2) concepts of child development with caregiving, (3) the physical and social environment, and (4) adult relations. Two chapters center on the environment: "Focus on the Program" and "Physical Environment."

Greenman, Jim. *Caring Spaces, Learning Places: Children's Environments That Work.* Redmond, WA: Exchange Press, 2005.

Good care for children depends on good child care jobs. This book describes in detail the high-quality work environment required for good child care and tells how to enlist the wider community to help get resources to reach those high goals.

Greenman, Jim. "Living in the Real World: Why Did It Turn Out This Way? How Buildings Go Wrong." *Child Care Information Exchange* 84 (1992): 49–51.

Design and construction problems in child care buildings are discussed. Common facility oversights range from too-small crib rooms and plumbing limitations to inadequate storage space and outdoor shade areas. This article offers suggestions for overseeing the construction of a facility.

Greenman, Jim. "Worlds for Infants and Toddlers: New Ideas." *Beginnings Magazine* (Summer 1984): 21–25.

Greenman, Jim, and Ann Stonehouse. *Prime Times: A Handbook for Excellence in Infant and Toddler Programs.* St. Paul, MN: Red Leaf Press, 1997.

This book describes how to organize a program of excellent care and education for infants and toddlers, how to staff a program, and how to establish and maintain quality caregiving. Three chapters address the environment: "Structuring Time and Space for Quality Care," "The Learning Environment," and "Infants and Toddlers Outdoors."

Harrison, Linda. *Planning Appropriate Learning Environments for Children Under Three.* Rev. ed. Watson, Australia: Australian Early Childhood Association, Inc., 1996.

This book contains suggestions for creating appropriate learning experiences for toddlers. It also identifies the nurturing role of care providers and includes a general guide to caring for children under the age of three.

Hast, Fran, and Ann Hollyfield. *More Infant and Toddler Experiences.* Beltsville, MD: Gryphon House, 2001.

This volume contains experiences that reflect and celebrate each child's development.

Honig, Alice S., and J. Ronald Lally. *Infant Caregiving: A Design for Training.* Syracuse, NY: Syracuse University Press, 1981.

This document is a clear, practical manual that answers questions about how to train infant and toddler caregivers to provide high-quality care for young children.

Infant/Toddler Learning and Development Program Guidelines. Sacramento: California Department of Education, 2006.

Maxwell, Lorraine E. *Designing Child Care Settings: A Child-Centered Approach.* Ithaca, NY: Cornell University Media Resource Center, 1997.

This manual is intended to help child care providers in child care centers, Head Start centers, or nursery schools design the indoor and outdoor physical space for infants, toddlers, preschoolers, and younger school-age children.

Moore, Robin C. *Plants for Play: A Plant Selection Guide for Children's Outdoor Environments.* Berkeley, CA: MIG Communications, 1993.

More than 200 plant species are listed in this guide, which describes the creative use of plants in children's play settings. "Plant function" tables detail how various plants can enrich children's environments through sensory variety, seasonal interest, shade quality, wildlife enhancement, erosion control, drought tolerance, and more. There is a section on poisonous plants and pesticides, a master index of plant names by function, and an annotated bibliography.

Nash, Margaret, and others. *Better Baby Care: A Book for Family Day Care Providers Revisited.* Washington, DC: The Children's Foundation, 1993.

Information on health, nutrition, and growth of infants and toddlers encourages and illustrates safety and developmentally appropriate family child care practices for children from birth to two years old. This book includes sample forms for providers. It can be used by training providers, entry-level center staff, parents, and *au pairs*.

Olds, Anita Rui. *Child Care Design Guide.* New York: McGraw Hill, 2000.

This guide can help architects and designers plan, design, and renovate functional and developmentally rich, pleasing centers. It contains step-by-step explanations of interior and exterior layout and design principles and case studies, licensing and code requirements, operational standards and strategies, and helpful checklists, charts, and graphs. Floor plans for infant and toddler, preschool, and after-school spaces, plus areas for outdoor play and more are featured.

Post, Jacalyn, and Mary Hohmann. *Tender Care and Early Learning: Supporting Infants and Toddlers in Child Care Settings.* Ypsilanti, MI: High Scope Early Research Foundation, 2000.

This manual describes High/Scope's active learning approach with babies and children under preschool age, including the organization of space and materials.

Schreiber, Mary E. "Lighting Alternatives: Considerations for Child Care Centers." *Young Children* 51(4) (May 1996): 11–13.

The author discusses the changes in her classroom that took place when she altered the lighting. She explores many issues surrounding the effect of lighting on people.

Stoecklin, Vicki. "The Role of Culture in Designing Child Care Facilities: Creating Culturally Reflective Environments." *Child Care Information Exchange* (May–June 2001).

This article explores cultural influences, classroom design, and cultural relevance. It provides support in creating children's environments that reflect the culture, values, and traditions of the country or area of the families served.

Szanton, Eleanor Stokes, ed. *Creating Child-Centered Programs for Infants and Toddlers.* Washington, DC: Children's Resources International. 1997.

The document provides a resource for designing a safe, healthy, and responsive environment for infants and toddlers (birth to three years) that offers ways to support young children's learning in all developmental domains and explains how to staff and evaluate a child-centered program.

Theemes, Tracy. *Let's Go Outside! Designing the Early Childhood Playground.* Ypsilanti, MI: High Scope Educational Research Foundation. 1990.

This book by a leading play space designer offers practical advice on providing a safe yet challenging outdoor environment, including step-by-step instruction on how to assess the play space of a child care program.

Torelli, Louis. "Enhancing Development Through Classroom Design in Early Head Start: Meeting the Program Performance Standards and Best Practices." *Children and Families* 16 (2002).

This article offers key design criteria in setting up and remodeling Early Head Start classrooms and facilities.

Torelli, Louis, and Charles Durrett. "Landscapes for Learning: The Impact of Classroom Design on Infants and Toddlers." *Early Childhood News* 8 (1996):12–17.

The authors provide guidelines for planning classroom space and selection of furniture in infant and toddler classrooms.

Torelli, Louis, and Charles Durrett. *Landscapes for Learning: Designing Group Care Environments for Infants, Toddlers, and Two-Year-Olds.* Berkeley, CA: Torelli/Durrett Infant & Toddler Child Care Furniture, 1998.

This comprehensive manual on the design of infant/toddler classrooms and facilities includes ideas on plumbing, lighting, furniture, and accommodating young children who have disabilities or special needs. Sample room plans are included.

Weinberger, Nanci. "Making a Place for Infants in Family Day Care." *Early Education and Development* 9(1) (1998): 79–96.

This article offers support for meeting the needs of infants and toddlers in the context of mixed-age groups cared for in a home setting.

DVDs

The Ages of Infancy: Caring for Young, Mobile, and Older Infants. Sacramento: California Department of Education, 1990. Developed collaboratively by the California Department of Education and WestEd.

Specific caregiving guidelines and suggestions are highlighted for each of the three stages of infancy: the young infant, the mobile infant, and the older infant or toddler. The 25-minute color DVD is available in English, Spanish, and Chinese (Cantonese).

It's Not Just Routine: Feeding, Diapering and Napping. 2nd ed. Sacramento: California Department of Education, 2000. Developed collaboratively by the California Department of Education and WestEd.

This DVD offers information about caregiving routines, procedures for health and safety, and carrying out the routines in a way that fosters learning and deepens relationships between the child and the infant care teacher. It addresses environmental issues related to caregiving routines. The 26-minute color DVD is available in English and in Spanish.

Space to Grow: Creating a Child Care Environment for Infants and Toddlers. 2nd ed. Sacramento: California Department of Education, 2004. Developed collaboratively by the California Department of Education and WestEd.

The DVD discusses and illustrates the role of the environment in facilitating relationships and learning. There are eight qualities to consider in planning an environment for infants and toddlers: safety, health, comfort, convenience, child size, flexibility, movement, and choice. The 32-minute color DVD is available in English and in Spanish.

Web Sites

California Childcare Health Program http://www.ucsfchildcarehealth.org/index.htm

Child Development Resources http://www.cdr.org/files/order.pdf

Community Playthings http://www.communityplaythings.com

Consumer Product Safety Commission http://www.cpsc.gov

Healthy Kids, Healthy Care (in English and Spanish) http://www.healthykids.us/

National Resource Center for Health
and Safety in Child Care and Early
Education http://www.nrc.uchsc.edu/

Project EXCEPTIONAL, Volumes 1 and 2
http://www.sbceo.k12.ca.us/~ccpc/
iccat/docs/projexceptrngdesc.pdf

Spaces for Children http://www.spaces
forchildren.com

United States Environmental Protection
Agency Information on Integrated
Pest Management http://www.epa.
gov/pesticides/factsheets/ipm.htm

Glossary

This section presents terms used in reading about how to design child care environments for infants and toddlers. Experts in design of child care environments believe that paying attention to these terms will clarify the suggestions about how to create an appropriate setting for infants and toddlers. Some of the terms, such as *accessibility, order,* and *organization,* will not be new to you. Others, such as *developmental barriers, mini-environments,* and *sensory impact,* might be.

accessibility. A general term used to describe the degree to which a system or environment is usable by as many people as possible. *Accessibility* means having clear pathways and easy-to-reach materials. For the teacher, accessibility means convenience, an environment that is easy to work in. For young children, accessibility means being able to get to materials and equipment and provides a feeling of control. When space is designed with access in mind, modifications for certain children with disabilities or special needs may easily be made. The key to accessibility is good use of the floor. An open space lets young children see and get to materials and other areas easily. Visible boundaries that create separate areas also aid accessibility. For children with mobility disabilities, visible boundaries can be very useful as long as the boundary does not prevent movement of the child (e.g., a large step). For young children, the scale of furnishings and equipment promotes accessibility. Water tables, shelves, toilets, sinks, lofts, steps, and platforms all need to be child-sized so young children can use them independently. When examining access for a child with a disability, consider modifications that promote independence and access (a water table on the ground while the child uses a vinyl-covered foam wedge as support). Storage also creates accessibility. A good arrangement of materials—in the feeding and eating area, in the playing spaces, at the changing table—ensures accessibility for the children and you.

activities. What children do with materials and opportunities. This term is different from the preschool idea of activities, which may have a defined goal. Infants

and toddlers learn and develop holistically and do not require lessons on topics picked by adults. Infants explore materials, people, and physical environments. They require guidance from teachers to help them stay safe and healthy and to help them learn to be careful with other people. They do not need, however, to be taught in a formal way about specific topic areas, as it is not the way they learn.

adaptation (also **modification**). The act of changing the environment, equipment, activity, or interaction in order to maximize access and participation by a child with a disability or special need.

adaptive equipment. Generally, a piece of equipment that has been modified or changed so that it supports a child with a disability or special need to participate in activities with greater ease. For example, a spoon may be bent so that the child who is not yet able to bend her wrist can scoop food and feed herself. A chair may have additional support built in so that a child with low muscle tone can sit without sliding forward. Toys fitted with tactile cues or sound can assist a child with visual impairments in identification.

aesthetic quality. The overall pleasing effect of an area. It influences teachers and young children. Some places make people feel good, and they respond happily. This is the response you should seek from the infants and toddlers you serve. Aesthetically pleasing environments are a blend of various elements: a few soft, warm colors; plants; the sounds of living things; comfortable places; and a feeling of order and harmony. Most child care facilities have a tight budget. You may be tempted to cut costs on aesthetics, but beauty has real value. The aesthetic quality creates the mood, which influences everything in an environment.

all children. Means infants, toddlers, or children. In some places, the word *all* is used to emphasize the inclusive perspective presented in this publication. (See also *inclusion.*)

boundaries. The edges of an activity area. Boundary planning involves deciding what activities and activity areas you want to have and where to put each one. Boundaries break up large areas into smaller, child-sized centers that are set up for certain activities. Boundaries give toddlers natural

limits and guide their behavior, tending to encourage some behaviors and discourage others. A boundary must be clear, signaling where an area begins and ends. To give these signals, you can use anything from a bookcase to a line of tape on the floor or a rug. Boundaries that also work as seating and as playing surfaces do double duty, a plus in a small center. Boundaries may be permanent: a wall, room divider, playpit or loft with railing, built-in shelf, storage unit, the edge of a rug, heavy furniture, or a counter. A boundary may also be temporary: cushions or foam rectangles, blocks, tables, light pieces of furniture, cardboard boxes, or an upside-down table. For the major divisions, use permanent boundaries. For quick changes in activity, use temporary boundaries.

children with disabilities or other special needs. Children with a specific diagnosis, as well as those who do not have a diagnosis but whose behavior, development, and/or health affect their family's ability to maintain early care and education services. The disability or special need may be as mild as a slight speech delay or as complex as a mixed diagnosis of motor challenges, vision impairment, and cognitive delays. Generally, this definition includes those children who are between birth and twenty-two years of age who are protected by the Americans with Disabilities Act.

control opportunities. The chances you give young children to make choices themselves about their activities. The more the children can choose how the environment affects them and they affect it, the more control opportunities they have. Examples of control opportunities are choices of what to play with, how to play, and where to play. The opportunity for control can also mean choosing to rest instead of play. For instance, the ability to

get into a private place lets a child control the amount of stimulation she or he receives in the environment. A child who can move freely, change position, create boundaries, and fulfill his or her physical potential feels a greater sense of mastery and control.

cultural sensitivity. An awareness of how one's own upbringing and experiences contribute to one's worldview. People tend to feel comfortable with what they know in terms of social expectations, foods, and comfortable settings and to see other ways as inappropriate or wrong. Cultural sensitivity also includes the recognition that other people may have different worldviews just as legitimate and valuable to them and that these differences must be explored in order to work together successfully. Cultural issues often come up in child care between teachers and families and between teachers of different backgrounds and cultures, especially around the issues of children's personal care routines. (For more information on this, see the PITC guide *Infant/Toddler Caregiving: A Guide to Culturally Sensitive Care.*) In terms of the child care environment, cultural sensitivity means becoming aware of the cultural messages of the environment (conscious and unconscious) and working to attune the environment to the families and teachers who use the space. It can also include expressing cultural responsiveness through changes in the environment that support families' preferences for their child's care, such as modifying a child's sleep arrangement to accommodate the family's preferences.

developmental barriers. Anything that separates children by making use of their level of development. The barrier works developmentally because the child can cross it when he or she reaches the next stage of development. Thus, a toddler will be able to climb over a low carpeted wall that an infant cannot navigate. Developmental barriers separate children with different capabilities but do not cut off the teacher's view. Developmental barriers separate younger from older children, so one room or playing area can safely contain children from newborns to toddlers. A low pile of soft pillows can be the developmental barrier. The pillow pile will stop very young infants and even crawlers. An empty plastic wading pool in which infants can play is another developmental barrier. Blocks, risers, a cardboard box, or a low wall are other kinds of developmental barriers. Caution: A child with a disability or other special need may have delays in the area of motor development and yet be interested and ready to explore in other areas. A developmental barrier should *not* interfere with access.

developmental challenges and risks. Physical, emotional, and mental tasks that encourage new skills. Meeting those challenges means taking some risks. For example, to stand upright, a crawler risks falling. Young children need to be able to take such risks. However, while they are trying new skills that are right for their development, young children do need to be protected from real harm. Learning to walk includes taking some falls—on a carpet, a mat, or a floor—not off a ledge. Toddlers especially need safe risks. They need to discover the right balance between risk and safety, challenge and security. A space for both infants and toddlers should have a variety of physical challenges. Horizontal nets, mats, mattresses, lofts, and wading pools full of covered foam pieces or pillows can all encourage coordination, balance, and climbing skills.

emotional tone. The general feeling created by a room or area. But it is not just a feeling; the emotional tone affects

behavior. Children learn what activities are acceptable in various settings. They get a feeling for the quietness of the reading area. They seek the climbing equipment when they really want to move. The emotional tone of an area should match its function. For example, the emotional tone of the rest area should promote a quiet, secure, relaxed feeling. You create emotional tone with pillows, colors, fabrics, rugs, curtains, wall hangings, banners, plants, aquariums, furniture, pictures, lighting, and arrangement. A soft, warm-colored space with lots of fabric suggests quiet or cozy activities. Active play calls for a space that has more color, hard surfaces, brightness, and openness.

environmental landmarks. Physical cues about location, boundaries, and shapes. Very young children remember the location of things. Infants and toddlers learn to use the main landmarks, such as walls, doors, large pieces of furniture, room lighting, and varied floor textures, to find their way about. They figure out how to get from one place to the next by using environmental landmarks, including your voice. Children who can lay down, sit, walk, and run live at different levels. What children see when they are lying on the floor can be very different from their viewpoint when they are standing or running. That likelihood makes the space of their world complex. A child looking for a ball has to remember two things: where he or she saw it last and from what point of view he or she saw it. A clear layout helps children navigate and make sense of the environment.

family member. Throughout this publication it refers to the people who are primarily responsible for a child, whether they are parents, grandparents, foster families, or others.

harmony. The result when the colors, light, textures, and furnishings work well together. Harmony is important to infants and toddlers because they are trying to make sense of the world. A harmonious setting is not cluttered or chaotic. It gives young children a chance to focus. A harmonious environment can take a lot of toy dumping and messy play without breaking down. A well-organized, pleasant, and ordered setting can be in harmony with the play of young children. Harmony is enhanced by simplicity— neutral or pastel colors for walls (one color),

surfaces, and background materials. With so much going on in the environment, a plain background is soothing. The children and materials provide the color and form. For example, plain wooden shelves are ideal for showing off the bright toys and materials stored on them.

inclusion. The full and active participation of children with disabilities or other special needs and their families, along with typically developing children and their families, in community activities, services, and programs. It is more than the presence of children with disabilities or other special needs in early childhood programs. When support, accommodations, or modifications are necessary to ensure full, active participation, they are provided appropriately.

inclusive practice. A term that can be used to describe the following circumstances:

- The interests, strengths, unique characteristics, and needs of *all* children are considered when activities, environments, and interactions are planned.
- Family members, infant care teachers, and specialists talk together about how to promote each child's belonging in the setting.
- Appropriate adaptations, accommodations, supports, and services are available and provided whenever needed to promote a child's authentic belonging.

infant care teacher. A term used in this publication to emphasize the comprehensive nature of providing care and facilitating learning and development. Infant care teachers treat caregiving routines as learning opportunities for the infant and set the stage for learning by providing developmentally appropriate, safe, inclusive, and engaging learning environments.

mastery opportunities. Opportunities for infants and toddlers to show their competence. A variety of developmentally challenging pieces of equipment gives each child the chance to be good at something and gives children at various skill levels different levels of challenge. You encourage mastery when you offer a variety of activities and activity areas. Easy access to activities, materials in specially planned areas, and child-sized equipment that offers safe challenges encourage children to master many skills.

mini-environments. Small spaces within a larger one. Mini-environments are used for special purposes: privacy, a quiet place to rest, a place to play with one or two others, a place for you and a child to relax together, or a place only for adults. Some mini-environments are set up for particular activities, such as water or messy play,

large-motor movement, naps, or sand play. Mini-environments are often spaces scaled to infants' and toddlers' needs. Small defined areas add flexibility and variety to a larger space. A large room with mini-environments reduces crowding. Set up mini-environments using boundaries. Create the emotional tone of each mini-environment with such decorative elements as floor coverings, furniture, colors, and plants. Neighboring mini-environments should complement each other. Put a quiet resting place far from a climbing/running area. Use the basic organizing principle of pairing like furnishings with like activities to set up different mini-environments.

modification. See *adaptation*.

multilevel environments. Spaces that have surfaces for the children above and possibly below the floor level. Multilevel environments are desirable for the following reasons:

1. Young children can get an adult-level viewpoint.
2. Multiple levels offer climbing challenges.
3. The play space increases.
4. The variety creates a special experience for children.

Multilevel environments include fenced lofts, climbing ramps, room dividers that work as sitting surfaces, climbing structures with platforms, pits filled with foam or small pillows, slides from another level to the floor, and floors with dips and hills built in.

nature and natural experiences. Breezes, sunlight, grass, sand, the smell of trees, and light on water—these are all parts of nature and natural experiences. Humans thrive on natural experiences, which soothe and refresh people. Natural patterns and variations provide gentle changes in stimulation, encouraging a relaxed alertness and inspiring feelings of comfort. Some experts believe the stress of modern life comes partly from too little contact with the natural world. Even young children experience stress. Experiences with nature can add to children's well-being and reduce stress. Natural experiences can include activities as simple as sifting sand, playing in water, and watching fish in an aquarium. The child care environment can provide natural experiences in an outdoor area that has grass, trees, and rocks. You can also offer natural experiences indoors with plants, animals, fish, and natural objects such as large, smooth rocks, shells, dried plants, and animal bones. Windows that let in natural light are another way to bring nature inside.

order. A setting in which everything has its place. Both you and the children need to know where each item goes when it is not in use. You can also maintain order by keeping materials in the proper activity areas. You encourage order when you plan a place for children to dump and sort—two favorite toddler activities. When you have order, young children can see playthings clearly and tell them apart, which lets them choose one thing over another. Children can also understand how order works by helping to put things back in order. Children who have a hard time focusing their attention especially need an orderly environment. Order offers clear signals about materials and areas. Disorder creates problems. Children and teachers cannot find things. A cluttered environment can overstimulate young children. In a disorderly setting, teachers spend too much energy cleaning up and looking for things. A play or activity area that is quickly tidied up has easily restorable order. Well-organized shelves, storage, and equipment make for order that is easy to recapture after a play period. Equipment

and materials that can go on shelves with space on either side enable toddlers to help clean up. When young children can help put things away, you have restorable order that also teaches valuable lessons.

1. Open shelves aid restorable order.
2. A limited number of carefully chosen toys and materials makes restorable order possible.
3. Separating activities and the equipment used for the activity supports easily restorable order.

Perhaps the best thing about easily restorable order is how relaxed everyone feels about making a mess. Feeling all right about playing and exploring—and making a mess doing so—encourages healthy growth and development. When you know a place is easy to put in order, you seldom have to say no.

organization. A system of arrangement. The arrangement can be of anything: space, materials, books, or toys. A system of arrangement creates guidelines that show where things go and why. For example, environmental organization would mean putting the wheeled riding toys in the large-motor area. Hand toys would go on a shelf in a play area. Soft, cuddly toys might go in the rest or quiet areas. The best organization is simple and orderly: items used together are arranged together—water toys near the water troughs, and art materials near the artwork space. Infants and toddlers are trying to make sense of the world, and organization makes the job easier for them. The children learn to expect certain things in certain places. Organization also makes teaching easier. When the setting is well organized, children can find things for themselves and help put them away. You can tell the toddlers: "The crayons are in the art center." "The block goes next to its picture here."

pathways. Good ways to ensure easy movement between different rooms. Draw a plan. Use a simple scale, for example, 1 foot in the room equals 1/2-inch or 1/4-inch on the paper. Measure the room, draw it, and add the doors, windows, and large pieces of furniture and equipment to gain a clear view of the pathways. If you cannot see any, rearrange the room, facilitating movement within the room and to other rooms or areas. Look for things that are in the way and move them. Paying attention to traffic flow is a good way to make life in the environment easier. When a child can either climb a ramp to a platform or go up stairs, you have alternative pathways—two ways to get to the same place. Alternative pathways offer choices, reduce crowding, and help make the space more workable.

peacefulness. An environment in which crying or shouting and noisy activities do not disturb the whole center, and conflict is minimized. To create a peaceful environment, do the following:

- Divide the space.
- Use acoustical ceiling tile.
- Consider having ceiling fans.
- Install carpeting.
- Use soft, natural colors.
- Provide soft furnishings.
- Include comfortable furnishings for teachers and children.
- Limit the size of the group.
- Separate loud activities from quiet ones.
- Make interesting toys and materials continually available.

perspective of the infant. What the child sees, feels, and experiences in the environment. Is the teacher responsive to the child's needs, abilities, and interests? Are family members made to feel welcome? Does the setting feel safe? Does the furniture fit the child? Does the teacher have reasonable expectations of the child's

abilities? Is the environment inviting and provocative? Does the child feel like exploring here? Think about designing the space from the infant's perspective. Try to imagine things from the infant's point of view. To do this, get down on the floor and see what the young child sees. While on the floor, also try to feel what the child feels and hear what the child hears.

pod design. A plan for an infant/toddler classroom that places facilities such as toilets, supplies, and food preparation areas in the center of a room. Usually, the facilities are separated by half walls or see-through plastic barriers. The facilities are available to different infant care teachers who are responsible for small groups of children. This design:

- Supports teachers in maintaining a visual connection and close relationship with children even as they conduct classroom management activities.

- Provides boundaries that keep children safe from bathroom and kitchen appliances.
- Is economical because more than one small group can share the facilities.

privacy. The ability to find space to be alone and comfortable. Young children in group care many hours a day need access to privacy. Private spaces allow children to be alone for rest or quiet or to deal with some of their feelings whenever they need to.

program leader. The hub of the infant/ toddler care and education program. The policies and actions of the program leader set the tone for families, children, teachers, and other staff members. In family-oriented programs, leaders create a welcoming place for families and draw family members into the process of reflecting on and planning the program for the children. Through ongoing communication between teachers and supervisors, program leaders work with staff members to solve problems and to improve the quality of care and education they provide. Program leaders ensure that the setting is designed and equipped to facilitate the learning and development of infants and toddlers and that the program's core policies support the growth of positive, respectful relationships.

reevaluation of the environment. Looking at what happens after a plan is put into practice. Reevaluation is important for child care environments because plans do not always work out as intended. The rest area may be too noisy. The quiet corner for cuddling may not be used. The realities of the layout can bring out problems. Reevaluation or ongoing evaluation means that you pull back from hands-on work to look at the whole program from a fresh viewpoint. Reevaluation creates room for improvement and allows your program to grow and adapt to new ideas or resources.

scale. Matching the size of an environment and its furnishings to the people in the room. That means the furniture, shelves, and equipment need to be scaled to a child's size. Appropriately scaled equipment encourages choices and aids growth and development because infants and toddlers can reach materials easily. When the room is scaled to the children, they can move about freely and carry out activities independently. Designing the environment to scale for infants and toddlers requires knowing the children's focus. The activity zone for infants and toddlers is 30 inches from the floor. Anything higher is beyond hands-on contact. Sinks, shelves, tables, lofts, steps, toilets, water tables, and platforms should all be scaled to the children's height in the activity zone. Scale also includes making adjustments so that equipment and materials are suited to your use as well.

sensory impact. Everything that is seen, heard, touched, or smelled in an environment. A child care setting for young children has to have a balanced sensory impact. Too much to see, hear, and touch is overstimulating. Too little sensory experience, however, leaves children with nothing to respond to. The children get irritable and bored and may turn to each other for stimulation, which may lead to problems and fighting. Things that change shape, grow, or move about add to the sensory impact of the environment. These objects include mirrors, plants, animals, mobiles, banners, and wind chimes.

storage. Shelves for toys waiting to be picked up or to be stored over the winter season. Storage can hold supplies used in changing diapers many times a day or cleaning supplies used once a day. Program flexibility is affected by the types of storage available. The more storage and the more types of storage, the more flexibility a program will provide. Plenty of storage is essential to a good child care environment. The best storage for the children's favorite toys is on open shelves with space around each toy. Shelving is much better than a huge box or bin with everything piled into it. Children can choose their toys when they see what each one looks like. To do its job, storage must be convenient. If it is not, you have not stored something—you have buried it.

variety. Choices about what to look at, what to hear, what or whom to play with, and what to do. The home is an ideal example of variety because it offers so many settings, textures, arrangements, and materials. A major example of variety is how the space is divided. When certain areas are set up for particular activities, the environment offers variety. When the environment meets the changing needs of both infants and toddlers, it has variety. Another example of variety is texture.

A child care setting can offer a rich variety of textures: the smooth floor, the rough rug, the porcelain sink, the wood tabletop, the nubby fabric on the couch, or the soft velvet pillow on the floor. You can offer variety for the senses by pulling the shades or using a dimmer to change the lighting, putting up new materials and pictures, playing different kinds of music or tapes, bringing in a large new plant, changing the toys, or offering a new art activity.